Let my Legacy Be Love

Let my Legacy Be Love

A Shortcut to Self-Loving

SECOND EDITION

CHRISTINA BEAUCHEMIN

WOODHALL PRESS
NORWALK, CT

WOODHALL PRESS
81 Old Saugatuck Road, Norwalk, CT 06855
WoodhallPress.com

Cover design: Asha Hossain

Layout artist: Sheryl Kober

Library of Congress Cataloging-in-Publication Data available
ISBN 978-1-949116-73-1 (paper: alk paper)
ISBN 978-1-949116-74-8 (electronic)

First Edition

Distributed by Independent Publishers Group
(800) 888-4741

Printed in the United States of America

This is a work of creative nonfiction. All of the events in this memoir are true to the
best of the author's memory. Some names and identifying features have been changed to
protect the identity of certain parties. Names, characters, places, and incidents either are
the product of the author's imagination or are used fictitiously. Any resemblance to actual
persons, living or dead, events, or locales is entirely coincidental. The author in no way
represents any company, corporation, or brand, mentioned herein. The views expressed
in this memoir are solely those of the author.

To my sons, Christofer VanWormer and Benjamin VanWormer.
Thank you for your feedback and your unconditional love.
I have been blessed.

~ ❧ ~

Author's Note

This book is a work of creative nonfiction. The stories within these pages are told through the eyes of the young girl I was at the time. Most conversations have been re-created based upon my recollection of events. No one who appears in these pages expected I would one day recount the events that transpired between us. The names have been changed to respect their privacy.

CONTENTS

SETTING THE STAGE

Blindsided? 3

Home Is Where the Hurt Is. 15

Open to Discovery 17

PART I

That's My Girl 27

For Crying Out Loud. 43

Losin' the Faith 53

Potential 63

The Fake Artist 73

Worth Less 89

Pink Bubble Gum Snow Cone 103

The First No 115

PART II

Chocolate and Carrot Soup. 131

On My Knees. 143

At the Falls 155

Thirty-Three First Dates 165

Again? *Really?*. 181

Making a List. 201

Checking It Twice 213

Just Love Him 225

A Deeper Meaning 239

Songbird: A Letter to My Five-Year-Old Self 247

A Thoughtful Walk to Forgiveness 253

Part III

Love as a Legacy 263

The *I Love My Life Challenge* 277

What's Next? 305

Finding Your ACE Score 309

Acknowledgments 313

About the Author. 317

Setting the Stage

Blindsided?

As the force of his words hit me, it was as if I were out of my body, watching the scene from above. From there, I could see the coffee in the mug he slammed down on the kitchen counter splash almost to the point of spilling over before it rocked back and then slowly became still.

"I don't want to be married to you anymore," Gabriel said, seething.

I was tired, worn down from the stress of the last few months as he'd thrown sarcastic barbs, stomped in and out of the house, and mumbled under his breath. I knew he was unhappy, but to me his complaints all seemed like small stuff. Leaving a pair of shoes at the bottom of the stairs or dishes in the sink seemed so minor.

I will freely admit that I am by no means a perfect person, and I was aware of the little things about me that grated on him. But in my exhausted state, I didn't question his words. Instead I parroted back, "You don't want to be married anymore."

His eyes met mine with an intensity that forced me back a step.

"You didn't hear me," he fumed. "I don't want to be married to *you* anymore."

I believe it was my confusion that caused his anger to diminish. He picked the mug back up, calmly added a little more coffee, and then turned to face me once more.

"Look," he said. "There's too much water under the bridge."

I felt the familiar wave of frustration, but this time it was quickly followed by a deep jolt of fear. This was my second marriage. I wouldn't let it fail. I *couldn't* let it fail. I heard the growing dread in my voice when I asked, "What water under what bridge, Gabriel?"

He rolled his eyes, sneered, and then stomped down the cellar stairs, shouting over his shoulder, "You don't get it, do you?"

He was right. I didn't get it. It had all been so good when it started almost six years earlier. From our very first date, we clicked as though we had known each other forever. He was so romantic, often surprising me with unexpected lunches at the office or sweet notes on my windshield. When he asked me to marry him only four months after our first date, he said, "I want to see you smile every day for the rest of my life."

"Really?" I asked. "Are you serious?"

"As a heart attack," he responded, reaching for my hand.

It was completely out of character for me to even consider making such a big decision after knowing someone only a short time, but he had brought a bright light into my life—a light that had been missing for so long. As I considered his proposal, I couldn't help but smile at the open, honest love that shone from his clear blue eyes. For a moment, I felt as though he were my knight in shining armor, and although I didn't fancy myself a damsel in distress, I was enjoying the excitement that coursed through my body each time I realized how much I already loved him. I had never experienced anything like this before.

Prior to dating Gabriel, I had been single for almost seven years. For most of that time, life had been busy and very stressful. While working a full-time job that involved international travel, I did my best to raise my two boys—one of whom wasn't handling my divorce from his dad very well. Add to that the house, the yard, the pets, the grocery shopping, and the kids' hectic schedules, and I was stretched thin—most of the time, simply exhausted. After having stood on my own for so long, Gabriel's passion for me was more than just flattering; it felt like a rescue.

Even though part of me wanted to jump at his proposal, I asked, "Getting engaged after four months is a little quick, don't you think?"

He didn't miss a beat. "It's long enough to know I've found the right person. I feel it, right here." His expression was earnest when he planted a palm at the center of his chest.

I studied him for a few moments and then leaned in to lay my cheek against his chest. "I feel the same way," I admitted.

He hugged me hard and then gently pushed me away, holding me at arm's length. "Get your shoes on," he said. "Let's go get a ring."

When he placed the beautiful, sparkling diamond on my finger, he smiled. "This diamond shines as bright as our love."

I can honestly say I had never been happier or more hopeful. But when I showed the ring to my coworkers, they glanced at each other before offering less than heartfelt congratulations. Only one voiced the concern I knew the others were feeling.

"How long have you known him?"

"Four months," I answered, forcing a bright smile.

"Barely," she said, her hushed tone stopping just short of an accusation.

Only a couple weeks later, after a glass of wine and a beautiful dinner, Gabriel had hugged me hard and whispered into my ear, "I think we should set a date."

"Okay," I answered with a smile. "Do you have one in mind?"

"How about next week? I called the courthouse today, and the justice of the peace has availability next Friday."

A wave of anxiety hit me so hard that it set off a flash of physical heat.

"Next week?" I asked, struggling to keep my tone light.

"Think about it," he said. "If we get married, I could move in, and we could share the expenses of the house. It would make it much easier for you to leave your job."

Once more I was touched by his eagerness to be a part of my life. I had been thinking about leaving my very stressful position for one that was less lucrative but would provide a better, more-peaceful home life. Upon considering my options, even though I knew finances would be tight, I believed the transition would be worth it. His offer to help with the household expenses would make it much easier.

But there were still so many unknowns. Besides the short amount of time he and I had known each other, I had another major reservation.

Her.

While Gabriel and I were dating, he spoke of "her" often, sharing that they had met just a few months after his marriage had broken up. "She winked at me from across the room," he said, "and then asked me to buy her a drink." They had lived together on and off for two years, but he assured me that more than a year had passed since he had last seen her and the relationship was over. Still, doubt had gnawed away at me. He was so passionate when he spoke of her, once even pounding his fist on the table as he related an incident that had led to their final breakup.

When he mentioned that he had run into her in the grocery store, once more I had probed.

"Are you absolutely sure you're over her?"

He had laughed, his smile broad and confident.

"Of course, I'm sure!" he'd answered. "It's not only finished, it's long dead." Then, to my surprise, he'd said, "I told her we're getting married."

In an instant, my tension eased. I quickly reasoned that if he still had feelings for her, he wouldn't have mentioned our relationship.

"What did she say?" I asked with a smile.

"She laughed," he answered.

I didn't like the way his words hit me. Confused, I asked, "Laughed? Why would she laugh?"

"Who cares?" he answered. "What she thinks means nothing to me."

I looked away, wishing he hadn't told me any of it. If she had no lingering feelings for him, wouldn't she have just offered her congratulations and moved on? He must have sensed my uncertainty because he reached for my hand.

"The past has no relevance here," he insisted.

But I knew better. My first husband had been married before we met, and although he, too, had insisted the relationship was finished, the unresolved feelings between the two of them had cast a pall over our sixteen years together. Try as I might, I could never measure up to his ex-wife. There finally came a moment when I realized I had lost myself trying to be someone that I would never be.

"But, Gabriel," I said, my tone solemn, "I know from experience that the past is part of who we are. It shapes us."

He smiled, his eyes sincere, and said, "I promise you that I will not do what your ex-husband did."

I sighed. I knew that it was just as unfair for me to judge him by the actions of another man as it had been for my first husband to judge me by the actions of another woman.

"Look, if you want to wait, we can do that," he said with a smile. "I need you to feel confident that you're making the right decision."

I pulled in a long, slow breath and then let it out, sending up a prayer of thanks. As much as I hated feeling pressured, I had been worried that if I suggested we wait to marry until I was feeling more comfortable, he wouldn't stick around. With his reassurance that he *was* willing to wait, a wave of relief rolled over me.

"Thank you, Gabriel," I answered. As the tension continued to flow out of my body, I wrapped my arms around his neck and pressed my cheek to his. "I think I would feel better if we waited."

He sat back and nodded, his eyes gentle. "Okay." Then, after a short pause, he added, "I just thought that if we got married now, I could put you on my health insurance. That would save you about six hundred dollars a month, right?"

His concern for me made me feel so safe and secure. *How did I get so lucky?* I thought as we sat on the porch and watched the stars twinkle above us.

Later, as he pulled on his coat to leave, he held me close and murmured, "Take all the time you need, Chrissie. You're worth it."

The next morning I was up before four a.m., after sleeping for only a few hours. Although Gabriel had assured me that he would wait, I knew he preferred to move ahead. He had mentioned several times that his lease was running out at the end of the month, and that if he renewed he'd be locked in for a full year. I knew I'd marry him in the future, so for most of the night my head and my heart had been battling it out over whether to marry him sooner rather than later.

It appeared that Gabriel and I had so much in common, and I believed that he was a good, faithful man, proven by his previous marriage that had lasted nearly twenty-five years. But I had only known him for four months. I had no idea about the day-to-day. Would he fit into the rhythm of the life my boys and I shared? I had promised myself years earlier that I would not allow a man to move into my house to try out a relationship, and I wasn't about to break that promise now. It was imperative to me that my boys understood the importance of commitment. Plus, I worried that they barely knew him. They had been through so much already.

As much as I wanted to ignore the issue of "her," I still had vivid memories of just how destructive it could be to a relationship when one partner is comparing the actions of another to those of an old flame. I reassured myself that I was much more experienced now; I was a better judge of character than I had been years ago. Beyond that, Gabriel had insisted that the torch he had carried for "her" had burned out long ago, and that he was ready for our relationship.

Then I thought about his offer to put me on his health insurance. Having him there to help pay the bills would take a big weight off my shoulders, especially if I decided to leave my stressful job for a more manageable position that paid less. It all made good sense. But was I jumping into marriage for purely practical reasons? Were we truly compatible?

As the sun began to rise, his words kept running through my head. *Take all the time you need. You're worth it.*

I had a good life. With Gabriel in it, it was better. I had never felt about anyone the way I felt about him. *A love like this only comes along once in a lifetime,* I thought as I sat on my deck sipping a steaming cup of coffee and breathing in the scent of the early-morning air.

When the clock announced six-thirty, I picked up the phone, dialing without hesitation.

"Let's do it," I said.

The first fifteen months of our marriage confirmed that my heart had been right. Gabriel was kind to my boys and me. He was light-hearted, he had a great sense of humor, and he was smart. I was so proud to be his wife, and he loved showing me off to his family and friends.

But that was then.

Now—six years later—Gabriel was insisting that our relationship was over. I couldn't consider letting it go that easily, so after a few minutes, I followed him down the cellar stairs.

"Gabriel, can we at least go for counseling?" I pleaded.

His answer took me by surprise. "I've been seeing a counselor for several months."

A shiver went through me before I said, "You have? You never mentioned it."

He nodded, keeping his eyes on the computer screen in front of him.

I sounded pathetic even to myself when I asked, "Can I come?"

He turned his eyes to meet mine, the expression on his face suggesting that he was considering my request. Sitting back in his chair, he lit a cigarette, pulled in a deep drag, and then blew it out as he studied me. In my mind, I could hear his defense of his smoking: "It's not a problem, because I don't inhale." With a sinking feeling, I couldn't help but wonder if I was kidding myself that he would be willing to work on our relationship just as he was kidding himself about his smoking.

As I stood waiting for Gabriel's answer, once more my mind raced backward. It had only been a few years into our marriage when it became evident that the torch that Gabriel still carried for "her" had begun to illuminate my faults. I could ignore most of his comments when he compared me to her, but when he started to compare our physical bodies, I began to shrink from the inside.

One evening, out shopping together, I tried on dress after dress in an attempt to pick the perfect one for an upcoming wedding we'd been invited to attend. I was fighting rising exasperation when, once more, he shook his head.

"Why don't you like it?" I asked, whirling in front of the mirror to admire the way the pretty pink dress trimmed in soft gold complemented my pale complexion.

"I hate shopping," he muttered.

Suddenly my frustration flared into anger.

"Gabriel, you told me that you went shopping with her almost every night!"

His expression rapidly changed to a sneer.

"You're right. I did like to go shopping with her because she looked *hot* in everything she tried on."

The saleswoman who had been listening to our exchange reacted without hesitation.

"You should be ashamed of yourself," she scolded. "This woman is beautiful." Then she turned to me and touched my arm, her face filled with sympathy. "I'm so sorry, honey," she said, her tone that of a young mother soothing a hurt child.

As Gabriel and I walked to the car, my cheeks were red and my downcast eyes were blurry with tears of disappointment. With the knowledge that he no longer saw me as beautiful, how could I walk beside him with confidence? At home, from then on, I wasn't comfortable being anything but fully clothed in front of him.

To make matters worse, she had started calling him for favors, and he freely admitted to going to her house. "She needs help" was his defense.

"Let her hire someone, Gabriel," I pleaded.

But the calls persisted, and he continued to go to her.

A discouraging session with Gabriel's counselor ended with no resolution, and I was not invited back.

Three years after Gabriel first announced he no longer wanted to be married to me, at my request he finally moved out.

Several weeks later, the silence in the house was suffocating as I sipped a cup of tea and tried to choke down half a bagel. My little bird Kelsey had died, and the absence of the song that had filled my house for the previous eight years was heartbreaking. I needed to go to my office in town, but I didn't feel like going. There was so much work to do there, but I didn't feel like doing it. I also needed to go grocery shopping, but all the decisions I would need to make there seemed overwhelming.

All I really wanted to do was go back to bed and stay there until the black cloud that was hanging over my head had rained itself out. But instead, with a quiet groan, I picked up my car keys.

Just then the phone rang, and Gabriel's voice came through the line, filled with all the genuine concern I used to find so comforting.

"You sound tired. Is everything okay?" he asked.

No! I wanted to rant. *Nothing is okay! I thought you were my friend. I trusted you!* My body trembled with the powerful emotion that ran through it. Taking several long, deep breaths, I calmed myself.

"I *am* tired," I admitted, adding in a hushed tone, "Kelsey died on Saturday."

"I'm sorry," he said, his tone soothing. "I know how much you loved that silly bird."

When the call ended, I stared into the front yard at the trees bending in the wind, the events of the previous nine years with Gabriel flashing through my mind. It was then that it occurred to me . . .

I am the common denominator in two failed marriages.

This critical realization is pivotal to my story, for in that moment I was suddenly and painfully aware that although I believed I was an open and loving partner, there was something awry in the way I handled myself in relationships.

I began to realize that although I had changed my physical address several times, in my mind I had never moved away from my childhood home, where I still lived with the hurt and insecurity that formed the basis of the stories from those early years. It was with this revelation that I realized it was up to *me* to change. This is where the real work began.

Home Is Where the Hurt Is

In order to do my real work, I first had to revisit the wounded little girl I had left behind many years earlier in a childhood house where she lived with eight brothers and two sisters, sharing one bathroom and six toothbrushes. Her two parents were stressed out, frustrated, many times volatile, almost always critical, rarely supportive, and sometimes downright mean.

> *Better a dry crust eaten in peace than a house filled*
> *with feasting—and conflict.*
>
> —PROVERBS 17:1 (NLT)

Open to Discovery

The original intention of this book was to tell a series of personal stories, all from a positive perspective, and then follow each with an analysis of what I learned by reflecting on the experience. I hoped that through sharing, I could spare my readers some of the heartbreaks that I had suffered. But as I dug into prominent memories with my friend Carlene, it wasn't long before we realized that there were shadows of something darker behind the stories I had chosen.

As my conversations with Carlene continued and I began to get a clearer view of the events that had shaped me, I also started to get in touch with the feelings I had buried for years. Each time an old pain was exposed, I learned to acknowledge, process, and then release it. With each new aha moment, my writings became more-accurate reflections of the events as they happened. It wasn't long before I had clarity on why I had been married and divorced twice and why I had always avoided mirrors. I also understood why

I am not a fan of organized religion and why I had been uncomfortable in relationships with women.

As I began speaking to groups on the topics covered in this book, time and again, audience members asked how I was able to detach from the stories that up until then had played such a large part in my thoughts and behaviors. Since I was curious about the topic myself, I started researching the work of several neuroscientists.

One critical concept I learned is that with a deep intellectual understanding of the many aspects of painful experiences, you have the opportunity to heal from the traumatic effects. Another crucial concept is that as a human being, you naturally react to your perception of an event rather than to reality. This concept is illustrated throughout the book, so you will have a good grasp by the time you are finished.

In 2019, my friend, Jacky Vimislik, and I developed a program called Breakthrough. It was through working together that I finally understood how to explain in simplistic terms this path to self-discovery Carlene and I followed. Jacky and I call it the "3 Rs: Three Steps for Working through Anything."

Step 1) *Reveal.* Find the source of an existing thought, which comes through digging into a prominent memory.

Step 2) *Release.* With the understanding gained through examination, releasing it makes room for change.

Step 3) *Reclaim.* Thanks to the brain's neuroplasticity, you can wire in new thought patterns to reclaim your birthright, which is a life you love.

The *Reveal* relates to identifying why some memories are so intense. The stories examined in this book are my most vivid memories. Some I saw as though a video was running in my head. Others appeared as very distinct photographs. For instance, in the chapter "The Fake Artist," I can see my ten-year-old self in shorts and rubber boots bending over a patch of yellow flowers. The picture is as vivid today as though it happened only yesterday. It was by closely examining this story, and especially *this very moment*, that I pinpointed the exact instant my lifelong habit of seeing only the good in people started. With this revelation, I was able to acknowledge the root issue, which was to shield myself from feeling hurt. With the deep intellectual understanding gained by looking at the event from a more-truthful viewpoint, I was able to release the behavior, and by doing so, I began to change my life.

The *Release* is a step-by-step experience that takes thoughtful intention. In our Breakthrough program, participants may choose to smash a piece of glass as a physical expression of letting go of an old thought or behavior pattern. For example, if someone realizes that their core issue is a bad body image, they write those words on a glass item. We have thousands of pieces of glass, but in many cases, people bring something to a session or workshop that has a personal meaning. With a word or thought written in bold marker across their chosen cup, saucer, or plate, they smash *with intention*. Because breaking a piece of glass to release an old thought or behavior pattern is not a daily event, smashing with intention leaves a powerful impression. As such, it is a singular experience—not one easily forgotten!

Once a feeling or emotion is released, the space left leaves room for a new, healthier thought or behavior. We call this step the *Reclaim*. Webster's Dictionary definition of reclaim is: "to claim back or to demand the return." This step is not only important; it is invaluable. Because so much is lost before a child is seven years old, many people feel this step is a claim rather than a reclaim. But be assured, it is a reclaim. You were born to live a life you love.

In our program, we use an art project to represent the reclaim. Each art project is meditative, allowing the necessary time to process the powerful reveal and then to integrate the energy of the release. Sometimes we have participants re-pot a plant and then paint the word *nurture* on the side of the pot. The idea is that building a new thought or behavior pattern takes time and attention, much like caring for a plant. Once home, the plant acts as a reminder to nurture the new healthier habit.

Another project uses pieces of the participant's broken cup, saucer, or plate as a totem. Filing off the sharp points and then laying the pieces on a board in a pattern that will act as a personal symbol is both meditative and therapeutic. The practice gives participants the thoughtful time necessary to feel the entire experience and to begin developing a personal plan for moving forward.

Although the 3 Rs is simplistic by nature, it is incredibly powerful.

As I said above, research shows that many of our thoughts and behaviors are established by the time we are seven years old. Thankfully, science has proven that due to the brain's neuroplasticity—the ability to form and reorganize synaptic connections—we can change negative thoughts and behaviors by teaching our brains to think healthier thoughts. By their very nature, healthier thoughts lead to healthier behaviors. Not only does the practice change your life for the better, but science proves it also builds the power of your brain.

This book is laid out in such a way as to help you gain a clearer understanding of the 3 Rs. At the end of each chapter, there is a section called *Discovery*, where I share the understanding gained by examining the story. It is important to note that I hadn't experienced many of my revelations the first time I explored the memories. Instead, as my conversations with Carlene continued, I uncovered more layers of hurt, and my discoveries evolved.

During this time of discovery I was always doing research, because I wanted to understand how experiences from my early life could still have such a significant impact in adulthood. It was through my research that I came across the Adverse Childhood Experience (ACE) Study, which was initially conducted in the mid-1990s by the Centers for Disease Control and Prevention and Kaiser Permanente. The information gathered using the ACE Test, a ten-question survey, highlights the impact adversity in childhood can have not only on a child's physical and mental health but also on the negative social consequences that can develop later in life. The information fueled my excitement and became the motivation for continued research.

Even with an understanding of the damaging effects of adversity in childhood, it wasn't easy for me to share my stories because I wrestled long and hard with the commandment of "Honor thy parents." Being a parent myself, I know that we do our best with the tools we have at the time. Parenting is the most challenging job in the world, and we receive no formal training for it. However, after much soul searching and prayer, and a heart-to-heart conversation with my dad, I realized that by sharing the insights I've gained, I am honoring my parents by offering a wider audience the possibility of finding forgiveness.

The stories that follow are broken up into three parts. Since research proves that many of our negative thought and behavior patterns begin when we are very young, Part One explores my childhood stories as a way to demonstrate how the child I was at the time interpreted the actions and words of the adults.

With the understanding gained, Part Two describes my challenges as I moved on from my divorce from my second husband, Gabriel. This section acts as an example of the patience and thought it takes to implement change.

Part Three is about you. The guidebook offers you the opportunity to use the same reveal, release, and reclaim steps that have changed my life. First, you can choose to revisit some childhood memories; there are writing prompts to get you started. Then you start the *I Love My Life Challenge*, a course that will open you to new possibilities. There is also an online element to help you along your way.

Even a small change in perspective can generate miracles. To make it even better, when you change, those around you also change. As they change, their family and friends change. The possibilities are endless.

I devoted myself to search for understanding and to explore by wisdom everything done under heaven.

—ECCLESIASTES 1:13 (NIV)

Part One

That's My Girl

I loved farm life: the fresh air, the huge trees in the front yard, and the smell of the mown alfalfa in the fields beyond the house. I loved the contented sounds the cows made as they chewed their cuds and the song of the barn swallows that twittered on the wires just outside my bedroom window. But as much as I loved all that, at five years old, I loved my dad even more.

I was born a sensitive child, so although farm life afforded me the opportunity to run through the fields and help care for the animals, those same things taxed my delicate system, and I was often sick.

"Daddy, I don't feel good," I said just a couple days before my mom's brother, Uncle Neil, would be bringing my grandmother for her annual visit.

My mother, who was tired from being up all night with my baby brother, flashed my father a frustrated look. He glanced at her and then touched my forehead.

"It feels like you have a fever, Chrissie," he said, using his special nickname for me. After running his hand over my forehead and then down my cheek, he asked, "Does your throat hurt?"

I shook my head, feeling miserable.

"How about your ears?" he asked.

"A little," I answered.

"Does your tummy hurt?"

"No."

After I chewed an orange-flavored aspirin and drank a small glass of water, he carried me back upstairs and tucked me into bed, promising to check on me after the barn chores were completed. "You stay right here today," he said, his tone compassionate. "You want to be sure you get lots of rest before Uncle Neil and Grandma get here on Saturday."

I cuddled into my pillow, holding my favorite blanket, and closed my eyes.

Thankfully, two days later I bounded out of bed feeling much better.

"What time will they be here?" I asked, barely able to contain my enthusiasm. The annual visits from my grandmother were always the high point of each summer. She was so full of fun and had the best laugh, plus she always brought candy and gifts.

But as much as I loved my grandmother, I loved my uncle more. The night before, as I had lain in bed on the edge of sleep, I had whispered a selfish prayer. "God, I would really like it if I could spend time with Uncle Neil alone. Just him and me." The year before, he and I had walked hand in hand to the creek bed, where we had searched for crayfish and pollywogs, and I hoped we'd be able to do it again.

As my father strapped on his heavy work boots, I pulled on my sneakers.

"Are you ready to go, Chrissie?" he asked.

I took his hand, and the two of us crossed the driveway to the barn where the cows waited to be milked.

Several hours later, my uncle's big car pulled in the driveway. He sat up tall, waving, his red hair tousled while my grandmother rode shotgun beside him, her pure white hair glistening in the sun and her face split by a wide grin.

When they had unfolded themselves from the car, one by one my brothers and sisters moved forward for a hug and a kiss. As my uncle hugged my sister, he looked over her shoulder and smiled at me before uttering the words that sent shivers of happiness through my body.

"Where's my Christina?"

I wanted to jump into his arms, but instead I moved forward with a few slow steps and a tentative grin. Another thrill ran through me when he lifted me off the ground, swinging me high in the air.

"Have you been good?" he asked when my feet once more touched down on the packed dirt of the driveway.

I hoped my mother hadn't told him all the bad things I had done, like getting distracted from rocking my little brother's carriage when I noticed a walking stick on a leaf under the big maple tree, or losing my red rubber boot in the muck in the ditch when I tried to pick her a tiger lily. But I decided that he would understand, so I nodded.

His eyes sparkled when he said, "That's my girl!"

When my mom, grandmother, and uncle filed into the house, I hoped to be invited into the conversation, but my mother shut the door, saying, "You stay outside."

As I played in the sun next to the big birch in our front yard, I suddenly heard the screech of metal on metal—a sound that was quickly followed by my father's angry voice as he yelled at my brothers, who were helping with the hay.

"He doesn't have the temperament to be a farmer," my mother had complained to my grandmother weeks before during one of their phone conversations. "He gets angry every time something goes wrong, and something is always going wrong around here."

A few minutes later, the rusty spring of the back door screeched in protest as my uncle pushed through it.

"Where's my girl?" he asked, smiling in my direction.

I rushed forward. "I'm right here!"

Extending three long carrots, he asked, "Do you think Fury is hungry?"

I nodded my head and then, taking his hand, led him around the side of the barn, where Fury, our Shetland pony, grabbed the carrots one at a time. Just as he finished the last one, there was another reverberating screech of metal on metal as the hay elevator jerked to a stop.

My brother jumped off the wagon to the side of the elevator where several bales had fallen, and I ran forward to help.

"Get her out of here!" my father bellowed, waving me away as though I were some kind of biting insect. Heat rose in my face, and

I dropped my head. "And knock off that crying before I give you something to cry about!" he ordered.

My uncle's hand on my shoulder pulled me backward. "He just wants us to be safe," he said in a comforting tone.

But I was crushed. I hated when my dad got so angry. When he was mad, he was scary.

"The elevator broke," I whispered, allowing a tear to run down my cheek.

My uncle brushed it away and then lifted me up, carrying me around the side of the barn.

"Tell you what, Christina. Let's go to the creek."

My heart immediately jumped with joy, and I glanced around, praying my sister was still inside the house with my mother and grandmother. As if reading my thoughts, he added, "Just you and me."

The two of us walked together, chatting about the upcoming school year.

"Are you excited about starting kindergarten?"

"Yes!" I exclaimed, letting go of his hand and dancing around his legs. "I can't wait."

I did have one reservation about starting kindergarten, and it must have crossed my face, because he asked, "What's wrong?"

I pulled in a long breath, let it out, and then confessed that I worried at night that I wouldn't be able to find my kindergarten room and would be lost in the big school.

"Oh, Christina," he said with a laugh, "you don't need to worry about that. Your mother will take you on the first day."

I shook my head. "No, she won't."

"Of course she will," he said, giving my shoulder a reassuring squeeze.

But again, I shook my head.

"She's too busy," I said, correcting him, and then added in a matter-of-fact sort of tone, "Plus, she doesn't like me."

He stopped in his tracks. "Of course she likes you. Why would you say something like that?"

I shrugged. "She says I'm going to hell."

"What? Why would she say something like that?"

I shook my head, shrugging again. "She said it's where kids like me go."

"Kids like you?" he asked.

I nodded. "Sometimes I do bad stuff," I admitted, once more thinking about my bright red rubber boots filling up with heavy, dark muck in the ditch.

He knelt down on one knee and then, lifting my face to meet his eyes, he said, "Christina, you are not going to hell."

Again, I shrugged. I wasn't too concerned about it because I knew my brother would be there, too. But Uncle Neil's deep red eyebrows furrowed in genuine concern. "You know God is good, right?"

I smiled. "Uh-huh." My mother believed that God was mad at us and that we should be afraid of Him, but I didn't believe her.

"Good," he said, standing back up. Once more he took my hand, and a few minutes later, we were at the creek.

Sitting on the big rock at the edge of the water, we pulled off our shoes and socks. Together, we waded into the chilly creek, the thick mud oozing up between our toes.

"Yuck," he said, laughing as I hunted for crayfish in the creek bed. As I continued my search, he settled himself on the rock and watched from a few feet away.

"I found one!" I yelled, lifting the crayfish high over my head.

"Better be careful," he warned. "That's a big one. It might eat you!"

I squealed with delight, dropping the crayfish back into the water.

A few minutes later, I pulled a rock from the mud, washed it off, and waded to where he sat. "Look at this fossil," I said.

The two of us sat, my cold feet touching his sun-warmed leg, our fingers tracing the outline of the prehistoric life forms crusted into the limestone.

"These creatures died thousands of years ago," he explained as he held the stone to inspect it closer.

"Was that before you were born?" I asked.

His eyes lit with a smile, and he answered, "Around the same time."

"Wow," I said.

Moments later, my mother's voice carried through the fields, bouncing off the bedrock and surrounding us with its echo. "Yoo-hoo! Suppertime!"

I pulled on my sneakers while he slipped on his shoes, and hand in hand we made our way toward the house.

My mother's voice was cross when she asked, "Where's your shirt, young lady?"

I dropped my head, embarrassed in front of my uncle.

"It's outside," I answered, my voice small.

"Go get it," she ordered. Then she added, "A young lady does *not* run around with no shirt on."

As I hurried out the door, I was confused. My brothers ran around with no shirt on all the time, and she never yelled at them.

"For God's sake, she's just a little girl," I heard my uncle say as the door slammed behind me.

When I returned a few minutes later, dirty shirt in hand, she commanded, "Put it on. And don't let me see you without it again. And enough of those tears."

"But I'm not crying . . ."

"Do *not* talk back to your mother!"

Now I was mortified. I couldn't bring myself to meet my uncle's eyes as I began to set the table.

As the scent of my grandmother's creamed carrots and onions wafted through the kitchen, I couldn't help but eye the bread pudding that I looked forward to all year. When my grandmother finished drizzling thin icing over the top, I asked, "Can I lick the bowl?"

My mother shot me a look and then said to my grandmother, "No. She's already too fat."

Just then, my father stalked into the house. Ignoring his obviously dark mood, my grandmother pointed to the bread pudding. "Would you like a bite?" she offered, smiling.

His reply was terse. "I don't have time."

He motioned for my mother to follow him, and he slammed the living room door closed behind them.

Once my parents were gone, my brothers glanced at each other, their eyes nervous.

Uncle Neil motioned me to him, so I climbed up in his lap next to my sister.

Several minutes later, when the living room door reopened, my mother's mouth was held in a thin line, her arms crossed, as my father addressed me.

"Christina, your mother tells me you talked back to her."

I wanted to defend myself, to tell him I hadn't been crying, that I was only embarrassed in front of my uncle and the embarrassment had tinged my cheeks red. But I knew better. And now my father was mad at me, too. I hung my head.

"You'll go to bed with no dinner," he said before grabbing the keys to the tractor and heading back out the door. "Let's go!" he yelled at my brothers, who filed out the door behind him. They would get supper when the chores were completed.

"Can't we just have a nice dinner?" my grandmother asked, attempting to smooth things over.

My mother's warning was clear as she held my eyes. "Don't interfere, Mommy." Then she said, "You heard your father. Get up to your room. Now."

All eyes were on me as I slowly headed toward the stairs.

Once in my room with the door closed, emotions washed over me. The barn swallows on the wire outside my bedroom didn't care if I cried, so I did.

Early the next morning, I was already awake and dressed when the door to my parents' bedroom creaked open. When my dad opened my door, I flashed him a tentative smile.

"Good morning, Chrissie," he whispered, motioning me to follow. I skipped to his side, and together we headed to the kitchen.

"You must be hungry," he said as he popped two pieces of bread into the toaster. He slathered each one with a generous coating of butter and honey, and then he moved the plate in front of me. "Don't tell your mother," he said, his voice kind.

"I won't," I whispered. It would be our secret.

After breakfast, as my uncle prepared to leave, he hugged each of us in turn, leaving me for last. Squatting down, he bent close and whispered into my ear. "I wish I could take you with me, Christina."

My mind bolted at the possibility. I glanced at my mother, who stood holding my little brother and speaking to my sister. Then I looked toward my dad, who was smiling and chatting with my grandmother. Feeling hopeful, I looked back to my uncle and asked in a hushed voice, "Can I?"

The shake of his head was barely perceptible.

"You need to stay here," he said, his voice low and his expression kind.

My heart sank. I didn't want to stay where my mom's constant criticism made me feel like I was a big disappointment to her. It seemed that even my best efforts couldn't please her. Every time she repeated the words *Children should be seen and not heard*, I wanted to tell her that children *can* see, and they can hear. But most importantly, children can *feel*.

Then there was my dad. He was so confusing. To me, the sun rose and set on him, but he was unpredictable, and when he was mad, he was scary. As much as I loved him, the only time I knew for sure he loved me too was when I was sick. I longed to crawl up into his lap and be his little girl, but I rarely did because I didn't feel safe there.

Standing in the driveway, looking into my uncle's eyes, I knew he *did* love me all the time, even when I wasn't sick. He was kind, and the gentle touch of his hand on my cheek made me feel that, in his eyes, I would always be someone special. He hugged me again, harder this time, whispering into my ear, "Christina, you are the nicest person I have ever met. There must be a reason why God put you with this family."

I wasn't sure I agreed. I felt like such a misfit here. But I also believed God was good, so maybe Uncle Neil was right. I would need to figure it out.

As his car pulled away, I waved my arm so hard it might have flown off if I hadn't been holding it with my other hand. In that moment, I felt like the luckiest little girl in the world because I knew that Uncle Neil loved me.

As his own family grew, there were times Uncle Neil would drop my grandmother off and only share a sandwich with us before getting back into his car for the return trip to New Jersey. I was nearly seventeen years old before we had the opportunity to spend any quality time together. That year he drove my sister and me to the Jersey Shore to spend two weeks with my great-aunt. I sat in the center seat so I could be close to him. While he drove, the three of us talked and laughed while I soaked in the warmth of his love.

Not long after that, though, he received a promotion that would move his family to Texas. I wrote him long, newsy letters, and occasionally he sent photos of his travels with a note reminding me to be good and have fun. Each letter ended with "I love you, Christina."

When I was in my late twenties, I received a distressing phone call from my mother, telling me that Uncle Neil had died. As I hung up the phone, I couldn't catch my breath. How would I ever live with the knowledge that he was no longer there, loving me?

My first husband Kyle didn't understand my grief.

"When was the last time you saw him?" he asked.

"Time doesn't matter," I replied, choking on my tears. "What matters is that I always knew he was there and that he loved me."

As the weeks wore on, I dealt with a grief that hit me like a hammer blow every morning when I got up and hung like an anchor around my neck all day. At the end of the day, I'd lie down exhausted from the weight of knowing that no one loved me, because by then I wasn't sure my husband did either.

About six months after my uncle's death, I wrote a long letter to his wife. I shared my childhood memories of him and the grief that still plagued my every waking hour. I feared my aunt would think I was silly because I hadn't seen him in so long, but several weeks later I received a response. I read the letter over and over, and although I no longer have it, I remember every word.

"Dear Christina. Thank you so much for the beautiful letter full of such kind words about your uncle. As you can imagine, I miss him terribly." At the end of the letter, she signed her name and then added a postscript. "He always said you were the nicest person he ever met. He loved you so much."

My heart was instantly filled with the same joy it had held the day Uncle Neil and I had sat on the rock by the creek all those years ago.

I folded the letter, tucking it back into the envelope as another wave of tears hit me, but this time I was smiling through them. Suddenly I saw myself as he must have seen me, swinging high over his head all those years ago. Once more the thrill of his words resonated through my body as the long-ago echo of his booming voice ran through my memory.

That's my girl!

Thank you, Uncle Neil.

Discovery

As a child, I believed that my mother did not like me. Her constant criticism shaped the adult I was to become: a woman with a poor body image who felt I was never quite good enough to be deserving of love.

Throughout my life I have had only a few female friends, as I believed women were critical of me, just as my mother had been. I was generally guarded and somewhat defensive in the presence of women, as a means of protection. Thankfully, I have since learned the true gift of female friendship and the special bond and support that come with sharing common experiences.

Through the process of discovery, I have come to realize that it was not that my mother did not like me, although that was indeed my perception. I now believe that with so many children in the house, my mother did not feel she had the time to appreciate a child that was so unlike herself. I have also come to realize that she was very unhappy living in a country setting where she was responsible for so many children. She had dreamed of becoming a singer and an actress, living in the city where she would be immersed in the arts. Instead, most of the time she was exhausted, often sick from pregnancy or recovering from having a baby. To make matters worse, she had grown up in an affluent area and was a complete misfit, living on a farm far away from the life she had loved.

What I have also come to understand is that I loved my dad so much because he could be very loving and caring toward me, especially when I was ill. It was during times of illness that I felt most loved by him. In order to maintain feeling love for my dad when he became volatile or was acting mean, it became my habit to justify his behavior by telling myself that he was tired or stressed out from so much responsibility.

Because this behavior was familiar to me, it became the model I would use as an adult in my relationships with men. As long as I believed a man loved me, I could justify almost any inappropriate behavior. I now understand that by doing so I was handing over my personal power in exchange for love. Making excuses for inexcusable behavior and disregarding my own feelings became so natural that I rarely realized I was doing it.

I have now come to fully appreciate that a father's role in a daughter's life is to teach her how to give and receive love in an intimate relationship with a male.

I have always believed that Uncle Neil's love for me was unconditional. He provided me a safe lap to crawl into, and his kind and gentle way let me know it was okay to be me. I have come to realize that Uncle Neil was the perfect example of a good, loving, supportive man, and he had all the qualities that are needed in a healthy relationship.

Let all that you do be done in love.

—1 CORINTHIANS 16:14 (ESV)

For Crying Out Loud

At six years old, I wanted to be just like my dad. No, that wasn't it. I *needed* to be like my dad. He was so brave, and he never cried, not even when our goat, Petie, butted him with his head.

"Ignore him," my father ordered as Petie launched at me early one morning.

I ran to get out of his way, but Petie zigged when I thought he would zag, and he knocked me into the wooden post. Hard.

"Stop it, Petie!" I screamed as tears of fear and exasperation flooded over my cheeks.

Not thwarted in the least by my shrieking, Petie backed up and prepared to have another go at me.

My dad gave an exasperated sigh and then grabbed him by the horns. Petie bleated his protest as he was escorted back to the pen where this time he was tied. As my dad headed toward me, his expression was annoyed when he said, "You need to toughen up."

Rubbing the tears off my cheeks with the rough sleeve of my sweater, I hung my head. What my dad didn't seem to understand was that, as much I wanted to be, I just wasn't as tough as he was.

To make matters worse, my biggest fear in life was of crying, since everyone around me didn't like it. I couldn't even hide the fact that I had been crying, for whenever tears rose, my face turned a bright, cherry red. I couldn't control the tears, and I cried so easily over even the smallest things. I cried each time I hugged a new batch of kittens mewling in the haymow. I cried out my heartbreak whenever any of the animals were sold. I cried when I was happy, and often I cried just because I was feeling so much love for my cat, Midnight.

As my father worked his way down the barn that morning, moving the milking machine from cow to cow, he lectured me.

"This is a man's world, Chrissie. You have to be tough. You can't show weakness."

I was embarrassed that I wasn't like the rest of my family, and I envied them. They were lucky because they were all tough. My mother never cried, and neither did my grandmother. My brothers didn't cry even when they skinned their knees, and when I thought about it, I realized my sister didn't either.

Still, I couldn't seem to help it. Just the day before, my mother had reprimanded my grandfather when I'd dissolved into tears from his relentless teasing.

He had stood tall, his face angry against my mother's admonishment.

"She's too sensitive," he declared, adding, "I didn't mean to upset her."

"Then don't tease her," she responded, her lips pulled into a thin line.

He had tossed me a disapproving look and then went out the front door, where he perched himself on a lawn chair and began talking to himself.

My grandfather was right: Compared to everyone else in my family, I *was* too sensitive. If I had been living in the world by myself, I would have loved being sensitive. Where my brother saw a newborn calf as nothing more than another chore, I saw a baby that needed to be hugged and loved. What my mother saw as a bothersome stray cat hanging around the back door, I saw as an opportunity to teach a scared animal how to receive love—and ultimately to trust. I loved how my sensitivity made my entire body feel. I just wished it didn't make me cry.

Feeling nervous but hopeful, I asked, "What can I do to be tougher, Daddy?" Since everyone else in my family was already tough, I figured I should be able to figure it out.

My dad considered my question as he leaned heavily against the cow he was milking. Suddenly his brown eyes smiled, the skin crinkling at the corners, and he threw his head back with a laugh.

"I know! You just need to grow some hair on your chest."

That doesn't sound too hard, I thought. I had lots of thick hair on my head. It was so thick that my mother insisted it always be pulled back in a heavy braid, and she constantly grumbled about how quickly it grew.

I pulled on the neck of my shirt, lifting it away so I could examine my bare chest. Looking back at my dad, I asked, "How do I do that?"

Again he studied me, this time obviously struggling against a smile. When he rearranged his face into a more-serious expression, he said, "Well, you might have to wait a while."

My heart sank. *I can't wait,* I thought. *I need to grow hair on my chest now!*

"*How* long, Daddy?" I asked, pushing down the rush of frustration that was causing my hands to tremble. With a cure for crying suddenly a very real possibility, I didn't want to wait even a moment longer than I had to.

"Oh, I don't know exactly. I guess you could make it happen faster if you drink black coffee and eat burned toast like I do."

Now we're getting somewhere! I loved to make my dad's simple breakfast of instant coffee and dark toast slathered with a thick layer of butter and honey every morning. I would just make extra for myself!

Later that morning after the chores were completed, I fixed my dad's toast first and then made some for myself. After placing the plates on the table, I pulled two cups from the shelf: one for him, and one for me. With great care, I placed instant coffee in each cup and then added boiling water, stirring slowly until the crystals dissolved. Setting the cups on matching saucers, I carried his from the stove to the table, making certain not to spill even one drop.

"Thank you," he said, not taking his eyes away from the paper. Then I carried my cup to the table, placed it next to my own plate of burned toast, and sat down.

First, I bit into the toast, licking the sweet honey from my lips. *Delicious,* I thought. Then I picked up the cup and blew on the hot liquid before pulling in a long sip. *Yuck.* I shivered, wrinkling my nose and shaking my head in disgust. *How does Daddy drink this stuff?*

For a moment, I considered dumping the coffee down the drain, but I quickly realized that if I was going to have thick hair on my chest like my dad had, I couldn't give up so easily. So, once more I lifted the cup and took another sip. The second mouthful wasn't any better than the first, but a quick bite of the honey-cov-ered toast diminished the bitterness that assailed my taste buds. There was no doubt in my mind that coffee was disgusting, but if it would help me grow hair on my chest, I would drink it anyway. And I would like it.

As I was eating, my mother entered the kitchen, carrying my little brother on her hip. I smiled up at her, but the smile quickly faded when she stared at the cup in front of me.

"What are you doing with that coffee?" she asked, her tone accusing.

I knew I looked guilty, so I turned to my dad with pleading eyes.

"Daddy said it was okay," I mumbled, peeling my hands from around the cup and dropping them into my lap. Only a few moments before, the whole thing had sounded like such a great idea. But as she glared at me, I heard my voice growing smaller. "He said that if I eat burned toast and drink black coffee, I'll grow hair on my chest."

She glanced toward my dad and then back to me. "Why would you want to grow hair on your chest?"

"Because then I'll be brave like he is, and I won't cry all the time," I murmured, praying she would understand.

She shook her head and then huffed out a disgusted sigh. "Paul, you really need to stop egging your daughter on."

My father tossed me a wink and then reached to pull my mother close. "Oh, come on," he said with a laugh. "Let her finish her coffee."

But my mother wrestled away from him, reached for my cup, and poured the contents into the sink. As the coffee drained away, so did my hopes for a solution to my crying.

Several weeks later, our family made the annual outing to the local county fair. With huge smiles and frequent laughter, we rode the merry-go-round, the Scrambler, the Ferris wheel, and the Tea Cups.

"Come on, Daddy!" I called when my mother announced it was time for lunch.

After a picnic of ham sandwiches with generous slices of Swiss cheese, we wandered through the exhibits.

"Can I have some cotton candy?" I asked.

My mother shook her head in a firm no. "You've had enough. Besides, you don't need any candy," she said, poking at my protruding tummy.

Embarrassed, I felt my face grow warm. But this was the fair, and she knew how much I loved cotton candy. "Mommy, please?" I pleaded.

"I said no," she answered.

I couldn't fight the tears of disappointment that washed over my reddening cheeks.

"Crybaby!" my brother said, taunting me.

Embarrassed, I countered, "I am not."

"Are, too!" He laughed before racing to the next exhibit.

With my head hung in shame, I grabbed my father's hand, and the two of us followed the sawdust-covered path to where my brother now stood in front of a small cage. Inside the cage was the cutest little monkey I had ever seen. As it watched us with rapt attention, it held an apple that it crunched, then chewed, and then crunched again.

With the monkey looking on, my father suddenly burst out laughing. Pointing at it and then back at me, he said, "Look, it's a red-faced monkey! And it looks just like Chrissie!"

My brother laughed and immediately chimed in, "Chrissie's a red-faced monkey!"

I was completely and totally mortified. My own father thought I looked like a red-faced monkey.

Pulling my hand from his, I tucked it behind my back.

Once again, I couldn't stop crying.

Discovery

For years, I struggled to get that red-faced monkey off my back. I was taught early in my childhood that crying was something negative and shameful and that it somehow made me weak. I learned that the only way to be viewed as strong and as less of an embarrassment to myself was to choke back my tears and do my best not to cry in public. Now I understand that feelings of shame and humiliation can play a part in developing fear, which in adulthood can become a barrier to an emotionally healthy life.

I was completely humiliated when my dad labeled me "the redfaced monkey," allowing my brothers to do the same. This was particularly painful because at the time of this ridicule I was holding my father's hand for comfort. By betraying my trust, my father unintentionally undermined my ability to trust others.

As an adult, I came to understand that crying is not shameful and can be a very valuable stress reliever in many situations. Unless I am in a situation that requires me to keep a professional or neutral demeanor, I am now comfortable with crying when I need to.

However, when I prefer not to cry, I practice what I have found to be an effective technique that allows me to breathe through my emotions rather than choking them back. When I sense tears rising, I relax my upper body and focus on my throat. I open it as wide as possible by dropping the back of my tongue. Then I part my lips and inhale. As the air rushes in through my mouth, I pull a breath through my nose at the same time, keeping my shoulders and throat relaxed. Generally, it only takes a few breaths until the emotion has been released. If you are prone to tears at what may be an inappropriate moment, this technique may help you, too.

I have learned that tears are the sign of a sensitive and tender heart. I now accept my tears as a beautiful gift, for sensitivity and tenderness bear the fruits of compassion, charity, art, music, poetry, and so many other wonderful things.

Fathers, do not embitter your children,
or they will become discouraged.

—COLOSSIANS 3:21 (NIV)

Losin' the Faith

This must be what God feels like, I thought as the wind switched directions. A summer storm had blown over, and now the tall grass in the field across the road was swaying back and forth in a wondrous dance. The thick heads of the timothy made a swishing sound as they rustled on their long stems, creating the softest, most beautiful music I had ever heard. As their song carried across the fields, I, too, swayed, a gentle smile covering my three-year-old face. It was then that a sudden rush started at the top of my head and then washed over my small frame like a warm summer rain. *Yes, this* must *be what God feels like!*

By the time I was seven, I was taking religious education classes to prepare for my First Communion. I loved the beautiful white dress, its sleeves trimmed with flowers, and the sheer veil that hung over my shoulders, reaching my waist. My smiling face was reflected in a new pair of shiny white patent-leather shoes in my closet.

I could barely contain my excitement as the day grew closer. Every Sunday in church, I watched with rapt attention as parishioners received the Eucharist. Most closed their eyes, a look of bliss on their faces, and then kept their eyes cast downward as they found their way back to their seats. I couldn't *wait* for that feeling.

"Saturday will be your first confession," Sister John Marie announced as our small class sat in a single row in the front pew of the church. "It's important that your soul be clean for the Communion ceremony on Sunday." I intended to do whatever was necessary to be sure my soul was as clean as possible, so I had prepared what I believed was a thorough list of my sins. That part had been easy, as my mother reminded me of them almost daily.

"You don't need a second helping," she'd say. "Eating too much is called gluttony, and gluttony is one of the seven deadly sins." "Did you finish your chores? God is everywhere, and He's watching. Laziness is one of the worst sins there is." "Disrespecting your parents is a *mortal sin*." Each time she said the words *mortal sin*, she knitted her eyebrows into a frown. She insisted that a *mortal sin* was the kind that left a black mark on our soul—one that even confession would never fully erase. And once when I burned my finger on the stove, as I stood wincing in pain she said, "That's nothing. Just imagine what it will feel like to burn in hell for all eternity." The thought of it still made me shiver.

As Sister John Marie surveyed our class, she asked, "Can anyone tell me why you will be confessing your sins to the priest?"

Nadine shot her hand up quickly, waving it like she was trying to hail the ice-cream man on a hot August day. Sister nodded sternly in her direction, and Nadine recited the words we had practiced on the bus that morning. "We need to have a clean soul, so that when Judgment Day gets here, we can go to Heaven."

Sister nodded and then scanned the faces in front of her, scowling before calling on Joe, who quickly looked away. "Joe, would you like to explain to the class what Judgment Day is?"

I saw him gulp, and I was grateful that she hadn't called on me. He opened his mouth to speak, his nervousness obvious by his stutter. "J-Judgment D-Day is the day we will stand before G-God to confess every s-s-sin we've ever committed."

"And what happens then?" she asked. Her eyes landed with a thud on me. "Christina?"

My heart jumped, and my hands trembled. It wasn't bad enough that Sister John Marie terrified me, but I knew she had no problem telling my parents if she believed I hadn't studied my catechism. Bearing this in mind, I answered her question quickly.

"He decides if we go to Heaven or if we burn in Hell for all eternity."

Her eyes bored into mine, and her mouth pulled into a thin, grim line. "*Correct*," she answered.

On the bus ride home that night, Nadine was happy. Her thick, blonde hair shone in the sun, and her red lips pulled into a satisfied grin when she said "I know I'm going to Heaven."

I was impressed with her confidence. I wasn't so sure I would be going there, and although I wasn't sure I even believed in Hell, I sometimes worried that it did exist. What if my mother was right? Thinking about how badly my finger had hurt for several days after

I'd burned it, for a moment I felt sick.

Nadine and I rode in silence for a few minutes as our big bus bumped along a back-country road, jerking to occasional stops to drop off our fellow schoolmates. Suddenly, her face darkened as she turned to me.

"Christina, what happens if Judgment Day comes before Saturday?" she asked, her look of horror causing me to react with reassuring confidence.

"You know the answer to that one, Nadine. If Judgment Day comes before Saturday, we'll go to purgatory."

I wasn't prepared when her face crumpled.

"But if we go to purgatory, we won't get to see God's face for a really long time! What if we *never* do?"

I realized immediately that she had a good point. After all, it *was* only Tuesday, and anything could happen.

"Don't worry, Nadine," I said with an assurance that I wasn't feeling. "Nothing is going to happen. We'll be fine."

With hopeful eyes, she said, "I'm so lucky you're my friend, Christina. You're so brave."

I didn't want to admit that, in this moment, I was a little worried, too. Saturday was still four days away.

When the bus stopped in front of Nadine's house, she hurried down the steps and then turned back to wave wildly before running to greet her mom, who was waiting at the front door. As the bus rumbled away, I thought about our exchange. She seemed calm after I had reassured her there would be no Judgment Day before Saturday, and her praise had felt so good. She was right: I *was* brave. I believed that God had made me that way so that when He was busy with people who had much bigger problems, I could take care of myself.

A couple days later, when I ran into the house after school, my mother was holding up the veil I would wear on Sunday. "Do you like it?" she asked.

I didn't like it; I loved it! I was ecstatic. Placing it on my head, I did a happy jig around the kitchen, being careful not to let it slide off my head. The flowers on the attached headband matched the sleeves of my dress, and the creamy white veil was perfect.

"Okay, that's enough." My mother laughed, pulling the veil from my head and laying it on the ironing board. "Go change into your barn clothes. You need to help your brothers with the calves this afternoon."

When I stepped out the back door a few minutes later, I froze. The sky beyond the woods was darker than I'd ever seen it before, and bright flashes of lightning flickered from the thick, brooding clouds. There was no doubt that something big was coming.

My heart jumped and then began to race. *It's too late*, I thought, remembering Nadine's face when I'd assured her there would be no

Judgment Day before Saturday. A wave of sheer terror rolled over me when I thought, *Neither one of us is going to see the face of God for a very long time. Maybe we'll never see Him.* At that thought, I did what any other self-respecting seven-year-old would do: I ran into the barn where my brothers were already waiting. If today truly was Judgment Day, I didn't want to see it coming.

Luckily the storm blew over quickly, so on Saturday I grabbed my carefully crafted list of sins before rushing to the car where my mother waited behind the wheel. Once in the church, I slid into the pew next to Nadine where she and I, holding hands, waited for our turn to make our first confession.

When Sister John Marie finally nodded in my direction, I marched forward, pushed back the green velvet curtains of the confessional, and knelt down. Taking a deep breath, I recited the words I had practiced over and over until I was sure I would not forget them.

"Bless me, Father, for I have sinned. This is my first confession."

Only minutes later, breathing a sigh of relief, I opened the curtains of the confessional and took my place next to Nadine, who greeted me with a huge smile. Three Hail Marys and five Our Fathers later, I was ready for my First Communion.

But the next morning was awful.

"We're going to be late! Come on, get in the car!" my mother ordered.

We can't be late, I thought, picturing the disapproving face of Sister John Marie, her long, thin nose and pursed mouth turned down into a frown. Hurrying to the car in my pretty white dress and shiny shoes, I was careful that the veil didn't get caught in the door. With nervous fingers, I picked at the pearls on the white gloves my mother insisted I wear while we waited for my dad.

Everything should have been perfect. The night before, my sister and I had helped my mother polish our brothers' shoes and hang their Sunday clothes. But during the night, the refrigerator on the bulk tank had malfunctioned, and a whole batch of milk had gone bad. My father was quiet, his face angry as he opened the spigot on the bulk tank and watched several hundred gallons of milk pour down the drain.

My heart pounded when he stalked across the driveway toward the house. My brother just happened to be coming out the front door toward the car, dressed and ready for church, when my father backhanded him across the side of his head, barking, "Get into the car!"

Not long afterward, smelling of soap and Old Spice, my father yanked open the driver's side door and jumped in. Throwing the car into reverse, he stomped on the gas pedal and we catapulted out of the driveway.

The little church where my class waited was about eight minutes away.

"Please slow down," my mother warned, her voice low.

A mere five minutes later we arrived, our faces pale.

"Let's go," he ordered, and we began to scurry out of the car. When my brother tripped, my father picked him up roughly, pushing him toward the door. "Move it," he hissed. My heart went out to my brother, but I was relieved when I hurried through the door just in the nick of time, averting certain disapproval from Sister John Marie.

As Mass started, I knelt with my class, and at the appropriate time we repeated the words we had practiced as a class with the entire congregation. "Lord, I am not worthy to receive you, but only say the word, and I shall be healed." My heart was thudding with excitement. *It was finally time!*

Together our class filed forward, and once more Nadine and I held hands as we walked. I felt so grown-up when the priest put the Eucharist on my tongue for the very first time. With my hands folded, I said, "Amen," and then closed my eyes and waited for the rush to come over me, the same way it had that summer day when I was three years old.

But none of it was as I expected. The Communion wafer was dry, and it stuck to the roof of my mouth. Panicked, I scraped at it with my tongue. Sister John Marie had warned that we should never let the Eucharist touch our teeth, so I was horrified when a piece came loose and then lodged itself against the back of my front tooth. I coughed as the wafer scraped down the back of my throat and, with flaming cheeks, found my way back to my seat.

I was *so* disappointed. *Where are the angels?* I wondered. *Where's Jesus?* My friend Kathy, who had made her First Communion the year before, had told me she had seen him.

I watched the rest of the congregation as they shuffled forward one by one, opening their mouths to receive the host and uttering "Amen." With their eyes closed, they had that look of bliss on their faces. What was I missing? Why didn't *I* feel like that? What did those smiles even mean? I had always just assumed that it meant they were feeling God. So why didn't I feel Him? What was wrong with me?

Then I had a thought. *What if they're just pretending?*

My mind ran to the stressful morning and the terrifying ride to the church. My dad had been so angry, but as soon as he entered the building, he had exchanged a hearty handshake and a wide smile with the usher who met us at the door. I watched my mother walk to the Communion rail in her beautiful dress, holding the hands of my brothers, who were dressed in cute suits finished off with little plaid bow ties. Our family looked so perfect to everyone watching us, but I knew better. We weren't perfect at all.

Then my eyes scanned the rows just to the right of me. Everyone else looked perfect, dressed in their Sunday best. Were they all fakers, too? Maybe they were *all* pretending about who they were; maybe they all went home and were mean to their families, too.

I felt nauseous when I thought, *Is any of this real?*

It was then that an even more unsettling feeling ran through me, and my heart sank.

Maybe I don't belong here.

Discovery

As far back as I can remember, I had an inner knowing of a greater power—of something that was so much bigger than me. The greater power that I came to know as God was loving and kind, always forgiving, and wanting only the best for me. I saw Him in the soulful eyes of the cows, I heard Him in the rustling leaves, I felt Him in the soft fur of a kitten, and I smelled Him in the intoxicating fragrance of the lilacs in the spring. But it was when I was alone and quiet that I felt Him the most.

As a child, I resisted the religious beliefs of my parents and the leaders of my church because their beliefs were very different from my own. They believed in a God who was firm, immovable, and punishing, and to them, religion was about rules and control. Their God was a God of divine judgment—judging us, waiting for us to fail, and expecting us to suffer. My God, however, was a loving God of divine mercy.

My parents' confusing and often hypocritical behavior taught me to be distrustful of adults, and ultimately, to be skeptical of the teachings of organized religion. I have come to understand that when we view God as punishing, vengeful, and waiting for us to fail, we live a life full of fear, shame, and guilt. This belief can limit our human potential, closing our minds to the incredible things that, with God's grace, we as humans have the ability to accomplish.

For we live by faith, not by sight.

—2 CORINTHIANS 5:7 (NIV)

Potential

I loved school. As a matter of fact, I was one of those kids who found great joy in everything about it. I loved my classroom, music time, the library, reading, history, and science, but most of all, I loved my third-grade teacher, Mrs. King. She was beautiful, talented, smart, and kind. She often said I had "potential," and for me, her classroom was like a safe harbor, a place where I felt protected, secure, and special.

One of my favorite things about Mrs. King was her passion for stories. Every day, just before lunch, she'd open a book to read to our small class. Sitting cross-legged on the rug, elbows propped on my knees, chin in hands, I let my imagination take me to faraway places—places I aspired to go. Many days, when reading time was over, Mrs. King would place a lined sheet of paper on each of our desks. Then she'd write a single word or sentence on the blackboard. "Now, it's your turn! Use your imagination to write your own story using this word," she'd say, pointing to the board.

Once we'd scribbled out our stories, we'd hand the papers forward, tuck our pencils back into our desks, and prepare for a restroom break before lunch. On one such day, as I stood at the sink washing my hands, Rebecca, one of the popular girls, came up behind me and bumped me with her hip.

"You're disgusting," she whispered.

I smirked in her direction as I threw my paper towel in the trash.

"Keep your hands to yourself," I countered.

She backed up a couple steps. "Oh, you don't have to worry about that. I wouldn't touch you with a ten-foot pole."

Two of her friends who were standing behind her snickered. I snapped my eyes toward them and then back to Rebecca. With a look of disgust, she glanced at the red, scaly, raised rash on my arm and said accusingly, "I heard you have VD."

As a third-grader, I didn't know VD from BC, DE, or FG, so I quipped, "Maybe I do, but at least I'm not stupid." She stepped away with a look of horror on her face.

The other girls ran screaming and laughing from the restroom just as Mrs. King pushed the door open wide. "What's going on?" she asked, her face concerned as she glanced between Rebecca and me.

"Nothing," Rebecca answered.

I shook my head, shrugged, and then followed my class to the lunchroom.

I was a little anxious when Mrs. King carried her tray to the table where Rebecca and her friends were sitting instead of joining the other teachers like she usually did. From a couple tables away,

I watched Rebecca whisper into Mrs. King's ear just as I bit into a wedge of juicy orange. Grabbing a napkin from the tray, I wiped away the juice that burned the scaly rash my doctor called psoriatic eczema, but which I called annoying.

Mrs. King was looking in my direction; the look on her face was troubled.

I should have never called Rebecca stupid, I thought.

After lunch, we settled at our desks and pulled out our science books. As we opened to the previous day's lesson, Mrs. King surprised us by saying, "Put your books away for now. I want to do something different today." There was some applause when she explained, "We're going to play a game."

We quickly followed her instructions, and the boys took great pleasure in creating the high-pitched screech that came when they slid their metal chairs across the ceramic flooring as we formed a circle.

Mrs. King moved her chair and squeezed in between Connie and Burt.

"The game we're going to play is simple, but I believe you will enjoy it. First, I'm going to whisper a secret into Connie's ear. Then, Connie will share the secret with Rebecca, who will share it with Lisa, and so on. Once the secret is shared with the last person in the circle, who is Burt, he will announce it to the entire class. Does that sound like fun?"

The excitement in the room was palpable.

"Okay, here we go," she announced. She smiled widely at the group before bending toward Connie, cupping her hand to her ear, and then whispering to start the game.

When Linda leaned in to whisper into my ear, I listened with intent concentration. I grinned at her and then took my turn.

When Dean whispered to Burt, Mrs. King put her finger to her lips.

"Before Burt shares the secret with everyone, I'd like you all to move your chairs back to your desks." The room was noisy once more as chairs screeched across the tile floor while Mrs. King moved toward her desk.

Picking up a bag of small gray and brown polished rocks, she waited for the room to become quiet. Then, one by one, she dropped a small rock on each desk. I picked mine up to examine it closely, noticing it resembled one I had saved from the creek bed on our farm. As I studied the shape and color, Mrs. King announced, "Okay, Burt, please share with the class what you were told."

He stood up from his desk, and repeated, "The tone to the left is Shirley Mandy."

The room broke out in laughter. Smiling, Mrs. King instructed, "Now, I'd like each of you to please put your stone in your mouth."

I was horrified. Why did we have to suck on a stone? What had we done to deserve this?

Most of my classmates looked confused but placed the stones on their tongues anyway as Mrs. King urged, "It's okay. Go ahead."

I glanced at Linda, and when she put her stone in her mouth, I followed suit. It felt smooth and cold, but within seconds, the outside coating began to melt away, revealing a malted milk ball. Applause and laughter again filled the classroom as each of us made the discovery.

Once the excitement had died down a little, Mrs. King spoke.

"What I said to Connie was 'The stone you'll get is really candy.' "

Connie nodded her head in agreement.

Then Mrs. King's expression became serious, her tone sober.

"There is something important I would like you to take away from this game," she said. "Today in the lunchroom, I heard something very disturbing." She glanced at Rebecca, whose face went crimson. Then she looked back to the group. "I need you to understand that spreading rumors is wrong. When you repeat a story, many times the story you are telling is not the truth. It is a lie. Rumors damage and hurt the people they are about."

Folding my hands and casting my eyes downward, I thought about a story I had repeated about one of my classmates just last week. I felt so ashamed.

Mrs. King dropped her voice, her tone growing more intense.

"If you hear a story about someone, do *not* repeat it. Instead, tell the person sharing the story that spreading a rumor is wrong." She hesitated, taking the time to look at each one of us in turn before continuing. "There is too much of that in this classroom. It will no longer be tolerated."

I glanced up just as she sent a sympathetic look in my direction. I sniffed back tears as a flood of love for her swelled up into my chest.

After a minute or so of uncomfortable silence, she said, "Please pull out your science books."

Several days later, Mrs. King walked slowly up and down the rows, dropping marked papers on our desks. "Excellent job," she said as she placed mine in front of me. Across the top of the paper was a bold A+. A feeling of pleasure washed over me.

"I'm so proud of you all," she said as she wandered back to the front of the room. Each student smiled, sharing the congratulations with those around them. We had all worked hard on the assignment, and it felt good to have it acknowledged.

Mrs. King continued. "There is one, though, that stood out from all the rest." Her eyes traveled around the room and landed on me. "Christina, would you please bring your paper to the front of the classroom? I would like you to read it out loud to the class."

With cheeks tinged cherry red, I stood up, pushed in my chair, and moved to the front of the room. I began to tremble, so she laid a comforting hand on my shoulder, applying a small amount of pressure.

"Go ahead," she encouraged.

I glanced at her and then at my classmates, who waited expectantly. Every eye was on me, so I began. When I finished, I grew warm under a resounding round of applause.

"Suck-up," Burt accused in a low voice as I hurried back to my seat.

I smirked at him and then smiled at Paula, who grabbed my hand. "Great job!" she whispered.

As spring bolted into June, the dreaded last day of school arrived. For many weeks, I had been anxious about leaving my third-grade classroom, but on that last day I was feeling the same sadness I'd felt on the day my cat Midnight died. I had loved all of my teachers, but Mrs. King was my favorite. What if my fourth-grade teacher didn't see the potential in me that Mrs. King had seen? Would I still be excited about going to school each day?

After we had finished cleaning out our desks and piling our books on the back table, Mrs. King suggested, "Why doesn't everyone share what they will miss most about third grade?"

I listened carefully to what each of my classmates said.

"I'll miss lunch," Burt declared, causing the classroom to bust out in noisy appreciation.

Mrs. King laughed along with everyone else.

"I will miss *you*, Burt," she answered. Then she said, "Okay, who haven't I called on yet?"

I looked down, not wanting her to call on me. How could I explain to anyone how much I would miss her? Then I heard my name. When I looked up, there was a warm smile lighting her eyes. I shuffled to the front of the room, my heart pounding. Once there, I stared at the floor, at first unable to speak, fearing an onslaught of the tears that were just under the surface. Finally, I admitted, "I loved this class, and I don't want to go to the fourth grade." I felt my face grow hot with embarrassment as the class broke out into laughter.

"What an honest thing to say, Christina. It *has* been a great year, hasn't it, class?"

As a tear slid down my face, I listened to my classmates' deafening cheers and clapping.

When it was time to go, we lined up for a final good-bye. I took my place at the end of the line, avoiding the unavoidable for as long as possible.

"I had the best year, Mrs. King," I said as I reached up for my final hug.

"Me, too," she agreed. One last time, she laid a reassuring hand on my shoulder, squeezing gently. "You don't need to worry, Christina. You will do amazing things in the fourth grade. You're motivated and smart, and you've got *potential*. You'll always be fine."

I hugged her hard, nearly knocking her off balance, and then ran for the bus as her final words echoed through my head and my heart.

The words she offered were a gift that has lasted a lifetime.

Discovery

Mrs. King's classroom was a place where I felt safe and protected. I learned to trust her because she consistently treated my classmates and me fairly and with kindness. Her dependably gentle temperament and genuine approval of me and my efforts meant the world to me.

In her classroom, I learned firsthand what it feels like to be built up through the words and actions of another person. She regularly praised my accomplishments and efforts, and she provided constructive feedback that always helped me to do my best.

I now understand that each one of us thrives on praise. Unfortunately, we tend to react more strongly to and remember the negative comments more than we do the positive ones. Studies on what is known as a "negativity bias" have shown that it takes five positive comments to repair the damage of just one comparably destructive comment.

The time I spent with Mrs. King in that environment provided me with a firm foundation upon which I flourished and began to develop a sense of self-confidence and self-worth. Because I felt as though she truly cared about me, I wanted to do my best and, ultimately, to reach my highest potential. Having a teacher or other adult figure believe in us can help develop strength, resiliency, and the ability to bounce back quickly from real or perceived setbacks and hurts.

Mrs. King's final uplifting words as I left her classroom that day have remained with me ever since.

Let no corrupting talk come out of your mouths, but only such as is good for building up, as fits the occasion, that it may give grace to those who hear.

—Ephesians 4:29 (ESV)

The Fake Artist

"Today you will be responsible for scrubbing the ceiling," my mother instructed.

I hated Easter vacation. While my friends got a break from their chores as they prepared for family celebrations that included company from out of town, big breakfasts topped off with thick slabs of bacon, and Easter egg hunts, my parents readied a long list of chores to keep us busy nearly every minute of our break from school.

"But I can't reach the ceiling, Mommy," I said.

My mother's voice was firm when she said, "You're ten years old. I'm sure you can figure it out."

"But how?" I asked.

"Just use your imagination," she said. "It's about time you started using it for something useful."

It seemed to bother my mother that I loved to search for fairies in the swamp by the creek or imagine friendly dragons living in the deep crevices in the bedrock out in the woods, but I didn't care. I turned my attention to the ceiling, happy that I was tall for my age. In the absence of a ladder, I pulled out a kitchen chair, carefully covering it with a towel, and then reached up, stretching my muscles as far as they would go. The bristles of the heavy wooden scrub brush barely touched the ceiling, but it would have to do. As I worked, water ran down my arms, soaking both my shirt and the thick T-shirt underneath. My sister cleaned the baseboards below, and the two of us whispered as we worked

Stepping into the kitchen, my mother reprimanded us.

"I don't want to hear any complaining."

My sister and I smiled at each other as she made a mocking face in the direction of my mother. Then we started humming our favorite song from Walt Disney's *Cinderella*. As I continued to hum, my sister mouthed the words that the evil stepsisters had sung with delighted glee as they watched Cinderella work.

By the time the clock worked its way toward noon, my belly was grumbling.

"That's enough for now," my mother said. "It's time for you girls to make lunch."

My brothers, whose morning task was to clean the heifer barn, would be hungry, too.

My sister pulled out a huge jar of peanut butter, a loaf of bread, and a pound of butter. I pried open the lid of a big silver bucket of thick, amber-colored honey. When I looked inside I said, "Mommy, there's hardly any left."

She glanced in the bucket, sighed, and then shook her head with resignation.

"It will have to be enough," she said, reaching for the tea kettle after depositing my younger brother in his high chair.

My sister and I laid out a couple rows of bread, slathering each piece with a layer of butter, followed by a thick spread of peanut butter and a very thin coating of honey. With practiced care, each sandwich was cut directly through the center and then piled on a plate in the middle of the table. After everyone sat down and prayers were said, I reached for a sandwich.

"None for you, young lady," my mother commanded.

My heart sank as she opened the refrigerator door to pull out a white bowl that she placed in front of me. "You can have a sandwich after you finish this cereal."

I stared at the congealed mass of soggy corn flakes I had poured for myself at breakfast.

As my mother had added milk that morning, I'd pleaded, "Not too much." But she had sloshed the bowl full, insisting, "You need milk." I had shoveled several teaspoons of sugar on the cereal and eaten as fast as I could, but in minutes the contents of the bowl had become a wet, sticky-sweet glob of mush floating in a thick swamp of milk. Close to an hour had passed before she cleared the bowl from the table. But instead of dumping the cereal out, she had dropped the spoon into the sink and placed the bowl in the refrigerator, saying, "We don't waste food in this house. You will have it for lunch."

Now I gagged just thinking about eating the soggy flakes that floated like reddish-brown lily pads in thick cream.

As everyone else ate, I studied my mother. I couldn't help but feel sorry for her. She seemed unable hear the music of the rain as it tapped on the metal roof or the song in the wind that moaned through the loose windows of our nearly two-hundred-year-old house. This woman, who on Sunday mornings entered church dressed to the nines and holding her head high, most days had a certain sadness in her eyes. To make it worse, the yellow gingham dress she wore around the house was stained with spit-up from my baby brother, a dingy slip hanging out below the hem.

As the table was cleared, I continued to sit with the untouched bowl in front of me. With elbows on the table and my fists packed under my chin, I watched the rain fall. It had been raining for days, dampening everyone's moods. My brothers were bickering among themselves, and my dad had been irritable, adding to my mother's unhappiness.

Finally, with a disgusted sigh, she picked up the bowl and once more slid it onto the top shelf of the refrigerator. "Dinner," she said, a determined edge in her voice. After wiping the table, she called my sister, and the two of us were assigned our afternoon chores.

"Into the bathroom, Christina. I left the Comet on the tub, and here is a cloth for scrubbing. I want that bathroom sparkling."

I nodded my head, glancing toward my sister as I padded through the dining room where she held a can of Pledge and a dust cloth.

A little over an hour later, I returned to the kitchen and reported, "I'm done, Mommy."

My mother sat at the table, the local newspaper opened wide in front of her and a cup of hot tea perched in her hand. To the right of the paper was a plate of bread spread thick with butter, and the smell of a peeled orange filled the kitchen.

"That bathroom better be clean," she answered without looking up, "because if it's not, I will get your father involved."

I wasn't worried. The blue interior of the tub was scrubbed, the chrome fixtures were sparkling, and I had even dusted the baseboards before I mopped the floor. As I replaced the mop in the bucket by the kitchen door, I wiggled my nose, breathing in the heady fragrance of the fresh orange.

"That sure smells good," I said. My stomach was rumbling, and by now I was feeling a little queasy.

"If you're hungry, your lunch is on the top shelf in the refrigerator," she answered, her eyes still glued to the paper in front of her.

"Mommy, I told you I only wanted a little milk," I said, struggling to keep a whine out of my voice.

When my mother looked up, she was resolute. "You are lucky to have fresh milk every day, young lady."

"But I don't like it," I answered.

"You are a farmer's daughter. I don't want to hear ever again that you don't like milk."

"Not in my cereal," I insisted.

Now she sat straight up and closed the paper.

"You will get nothing else to eat until you have eaten that cereal. Do you understand?"

Our eyes locked, but I said nothing. When she turned back to the paper, she reached down for a slice of bread, bit into it, and then licked the thick butter off her lips. Glancing up, she asked,

"Do you need something else to do?"

I shook my head and left the kitchen, climbing the stairs to my bedroom where my sister sat watching the rain pelt the barn swallows on the wire outside.

"We shouldn't have to spend the entire vacation cleaning," she grumbled.

Although I agreed with her, I said, "We need to help. Mommy's tired."

She sniffed, turning her nose up in disgust. "We're not the ones who wanted to have so many kids. Besides, we're not slaves."

I raised my fingers to my lips and glanced toward the door. "Shhh," I whispered. "You don't want her to hear us, do you?"

"Why not?" she answered, shaking her hair off her shoulders. "It's the truth."

Sighing, I grabbed a book and then flopped onto my stomach on the bed.

"You're always hiding behind your stupid stories," she said accusingly.

I shrugged, turning my eyes back to the page in front of me. My sister didn't seem to understand that I lived for the stories of heroines in history—brave women who weren't afraid to speak their minds.

As I read, the dark clouds began to turn a lighter gray, and a hint of sun played just out of sight. The door across the hallway from our bedroom opened and then closed, signaling that my mother would be occupied for at least thirty minutes feeding our baby brother. I quietly tiptoed past her door, careful to avoid the creaky step, and then hurried to the kitchen, where I pulled on my green rubber boots.

Pushing the back door open, I glanced around. The yard was empty, so I hurried unnoticed toward the lane that led to the creek. As I walked, I stopped intermittently to close my eyes and open my mouth, tasting the lingering mist as it covered my tongue. When I came over the small ridge just a few feet from the swamp, my eyes opened wide as my brain photographed the magical scene in front of me.

Yellow flowers, everywhere! The entire swamp was in bloom! Broad green leaves hugged lush circles of the brightest yellow I had ever seen. Running forward to breathe in the earthy smell of the murky marsh, I bent down to inspect them closer. All my senses took in their beauty, and as my mind and body reveled in the glorious scene, I made a pact with myself never to let the magic in that moment go.

After several minutes, I looked away, and it was then that I saw sunbeams. Beam after beam of soft yellow light sliced down through the thick gray clouds, lighting up the muddy fields with a warm glow. I hugged myself hard, wishing I could stop time so I could stay right there in that moment forever.

But time *did* move on, and by the time I was fourteen, the list of chores was longer than ever. By then our family had been completed with the birth of my youngest brother more than a year earlier. Right after he was born, my parents bought a much larger farm. The place was a grand old house with four bathrooms, five bedrooms, a winding staircase, a huge kitchen with a butler's pantry, and the coolest attic I had ever seen. I spent a good portion of my free time exploring that attic, happily sorting through the treasures left there by the previous owner.

But my mother was not happy, and the stress my father was under trying to run such a huge farm with only the help of my brothers and me began to erupt more and more often into violent outbursts.

"Go in the house and help your mother," my father commanded one hot afternoon after I had just finished helping my brothers load in a wagon of hay. My resentment rose, and I huffed out a breath. It was becoming an issue for me that I was expected to work as hard as my brothers, who had only barn chores, and then go work with my sister, who had only house chores.

"Don't you roll your eyes at me," he warned.

"I didn't," I answered, feeling a wave of dread run through me. Lately his violent outbursts had become more frightening, so I was careful to avoid doing anything that would anger him.

"Get moving," he ordered as he jumped back up on the tractor.

His backward glance as he drove off caused me to hurry toward the house, where I could hear my mother and sister arguing. Once more I sighed, this time in resigned exasperation. All I wanted was a little peace, but at thirteen, my already outspoken younger sister was becoming rebellious.

"We're not the ones who wanted all these kids," she fumed.

"Why should I have no life just because you don't have one?"

Just shut up, I thought.

As I hung my jacket on the hook by the door, my mother turned to me. "Chrissie, you and your sister get upstairs and get busy." Pointing to me, she said, "You get those bathrooms cleaned." Then, nodding in my sister's direction, she instructed, "And you can make the beds and put the laundry away."

As we moved up the winding staircase, my sister grumbled, "We should have some time off on Saturday." When I didn't respond, she asked, "Don't you think so?"

I looked at her, shrugged my shoulders, and went to the linen closet to grab the cleaning supplies.

"I hate you," she hissed.

Later that afternoon, the chores completed, the two of us snuck out the back door, crossed the side fields, and headed down the road to where the Spieglers, an old couple who had survived Auschwitz, lived.

"We saw terrible things," Mrs. Spiegler had said on several occasions. "But we stayed out of the way, and we were able to survive."

"We were the lucky ones," her husband said, nodding and looking deep into Mrs. Spiegler's eyes.

After sharing a cup of tea, I explained, "We can't stay. We're not supposed to bother you."

Mrs. Spiegler hugged me hard as we moved toward the door. "But we love when you visit. Come again soon."

Once outside, my sister and I walked toward the road where we perched ourselves on the railed fence along the highway. My sister chatted about her boyfriend while I soaked in the beauty of the greenery along the Susquehanna River.

We had only been there a few minutes when the family car came racing in our direction.

"Uh-oh," I said.

My dad's face was angry when he rolled down the window. "Get in," he ordered.

My heart was pounding hard in my chest. *We shouldn't have come*, I mouthed to my sister.

"What were you doing down here?" my dad asked as he slammed his foot down on the accelerator.

"Nothing," I answered. "We just stopped in to see the Spieglers."

The smoldering anger in his eyes when he looked at me in the rearview mirror made my heart pound harder still.

"How dare you lie to me?" he said accusingly.

Confused, I answered, "But, Daddy, I'm not lying. We had tea with the Spieglers. You can ask—"

"Yes, you are," he insisted. "I saw you waving at that truck."

I shook my head, confused by his anger. "He blew his horn at us," I explained.

"So you're admitting that you lied," he countered.

Now I was baffled. Truck drivers flew by our house all the time, blowing their horns and adding a friendly wave. My dad had waved at them himself.

"But, Daddy," I said, "we were talking, and when the truck driver blew his horn, we waved."

By now he had pulled into our driveway, slamming on the

brakes so hard that we flew forward.

"Get out," he ordered. He stood waiting in a challenging stance as we climbed out of the backseat. When I walked past him, he said, "No daughter of mine is going to be a tramp or a floozy."

Even more mystified, I said, "But I'm not—"

It was then that his fist flew out, connecting with my face. Bright stars burst in front of my eyes, and blood gushed out of my nose, staining the front of my shirt. "Don't you ever let me catch you waving at a truck driver again."

In shock, I backed away and moved toward the house.

"Get in there and help your mother," he snarled.

My mother, who had witnessed the exchange through the open window, glanced up from the dishes with a tight-lipped smile. "You get what you deserve," she sniffed, lifting a sudsy plate from the sink.

After washing my face, taking care not to touch my swollen nose, I sat on the edge of the bed while my sister ranted.

"He needs to keep his hands to himself. He has no right to touch us!"

My head was hurting, and I wished she would just be quiet, so I said, "He's just so stressed out."

My sister spat right back, "Don't you defend him."

But I wasn't as angry with my dad as I was with my mother. "What I wish is that Mommy would stop complaining all the time. She just gets him madder."

My sister's expression was disbelieving. "He just punched you." I shrugged as tears filled my eyes. Her tone was incredulous when she asked, "You mean you're going to sit there and tell me this doesn't make you angry?"

I *was* angry, but right there, in that moment, I was also powerless. I loved my dad so much, but since we had moved to the new farm, he was angrier and more prone to violence than he'd ever been before. His moods turned from happy to aggressive so quickly there was no time to get out of his way. What he had done was wrong; I knew that. But being angry wasn't going to help anything, and standing up to him would just cause more problems.

And then there was my mother. She was constantly fueling him. We lived in a beautiful house, but all she ever did was complain about it. And no matter how much we did to help, it was never enough for her. My dad was completely stressed out, so if it made him feel better to hit me, then I would have to be all right with it. It was only four more years until I was eighteen and could leave. Until then, I would do my best to keep my head down and stay out of the way.

When I finally met my sister's eyes, I answered her question with just a slight shake of my head. She became incensed. "You are such a *fake artist!* Why can't you ever just be honest?"

What good would it do? I thought as a wave of extreme sadness rolled over me.

With disgust, she pursed her mouth into a prissy expression, imitating a conversation between my dad and me. "Oh, don't worry, Daddy. It's okay. As long as you feel better, that's all that counts." She sneered again. "You are such a *liar.* You make me physically sick to my stomach."

Pacing back and forth, her fists clenched, she asked, "Do you know what really makes me hate you even more? It's that you've perfected this whole fake artist role so well you don't even know you're doing it anymore."

"I'm just trying to stay out of the way," I answered, desperately clinging to the image in my mind of the yellow flowers, the sunbeams, and the way I felt that day in the swamp four years earlier. "I just want peace. I'm trying to have a nice life."

"Well, good luck with that," she spewed back.

I couldn't admit that I envied her willingness to stand up to both of our parents. My own sister was like one of those brave women I so loved to read about. But her courage also disrupted the little peace we had in the house, so in that respect I hated it.

Several months later, my parents sold the farm, and once more we packed up the animals, the machinery, and all thirteen of us and moved back to the smaller house, with just one bathroom.

Early one morning soon afterward, I found my mother sitting at the kitchen table, a cup of coffee in her hand, staring dreamily out the big windows. When she turned to meet my eyes, she looked so content. "Doesn't it feel wonderful to be home?" she asked.

I scanned the dingy blue kitchen, which had suffered more than the usual amount of wear and tear from the family that had rented it for two years. I missed my sunny bedroom, the spacious living room, and the four bathrooms. I hated this house, and more than that, I hated returning to my old life where distance from town made it difficult to be involved in school activities. I wanted to tell her how much I detested the entire situation, but because I could see how happy she was, instead I said, "It *is* nice to be back, Mommy."

Fake artist.

My sister was right.

Discovery

As a kid, I had the ability to make demoralizing and extremely stressful conditions okay with me. Throughout my life, I made a practice of finding the yellow flowers in every situation. As a result, I was rarely able to see anything as it truly was. Instead, I saw what I *hoped* to see because it made me feel better.

I learned at an early age to mentally separate myself from most negative feelings, choosing to find the good and positive side in everything. What I did not understand was that by discounting my feelings—or in many cases, completely disregarding my own wants and needs—I allowed others to treat me poorly. In cases where I was forced to see the worst in people, I rationalized their behavior as a means to excuse it. I did not realize that by doing so I was giving away my personal power, thus muddying the boundaries between what is acceptable and what is not. As a result, I allowed people, circumstances, and situations that were unacceptable to play an active role in my life.

When it came to my parents, I transferred any negative feelings about my dad, who I adored, to my mother, because I didn't believe she even *liked* me, let alone *loved* me. As a way to not feel so alone in the world, I needed the love of a parent, and in my mind, my dad was the only one available.

By the time I was ten years old, I had found shelter in the idea of the yellow flowers and the knowledge that I would be able to escape my home when I was eighteen years old.

So stop telling lies. Let us tell our neighbors the truth,
for we are all parts of the same body.

—Ephesians 4:25 (NLT)

Worth Less

As the feeling of dread grew, I couldn't seem to tear my eyes away from the big clock on the wall. The bright white face was in sharp contrast to the thick black hands that seemed to move more quickly as they counted down the seconds that remained until two o'clock. Tick. Tick. Tick. Normally I found comfort in the rhythm of the day as the clock shepherded us first toward lunch break, then to reading group, and finally, to free time. But today, the sound was more like an unrelenting taunt. Tick. Tick! *Tick!!*

Maybe she'll forget, I thought. For a moment, I was hopeful. My fourth-grade teacher was bent over a thick stack of book reports, her red pen scratching over the pages. For a few seconds, I studied her. I was so lucky that Mrs. King had moved up a grade to teach our class and that I was in her room again. I enjoyed every single minute of every day . . . every day, that is, except today.

Stop staring at her! I thought. *She'll notice!*

I promptly averted my eyes and settled them on the page in front of me, but the words dissolved into a muddy puddle, leaving the story lost in the muck.

Once more I looked up, this time surveying the room where most of my classmates were relaxed, leaning comfortably on their desks, some with their elbows propped up, head in hand. As usual, Burt was looking out the window. Suddenly, he turned his head, catching my eye. *You stink*, he mouthed, grinning and holding his nose. I smirked, shook my head, and stuck out my tongue.

It was then that my teacher looked up from her work.

"Christina, it's time for your dentist appointment," she said with a pleasant smile.

Drawing in a huge breath before releasing it with an even bigger sigh, I stood up, giving an award-winning performance of calm and confidence. As I slid on my coat, she said, "Officer Dave will meet you outside to walk you across the road."

I nodded, and as I stepped out into the hallway, she called, "Christina, button up your coat, please. It's cold out there!" I forced a smile but decided I would ignore her advice. If I were lucky, I would freeze to death on the way.

As promised, Officer Dave, our town's police department of one, met me at the intersection in front of the school, his cheeks brushed red by the brisk cold.

"Where are your gloves?" he asked.

"I don't have any," I answered.

He shook his head, rubbed my cold hands with his, and

then escorted me to the dentist's office. "I'll be right here when you're finished," he promised, and with a salute, added, "Tell the doc I said hello."

Shoving the door inward, I stepped into the vestibule and began the steep climb up the hollow-sounding wooden steps to the second-floor office. Thump. Thump. Thump.

Just as I reached the landing, the pretty dental assistant with blonde hair and wire-framed glasses opened the door.

"There you are, Christina!" she said in greeting. "The doctor is just getting things ready for you, so make yourself comfortable. I'll be out to get you soon."

As I hung my coat on the hook by the desk, I surveyed the empty waiting area. My heart was pounding so hard that I could see the front of my blouse vibrating with the heavy beat.

The room was furnished with blue chairs placed against blue walls accented by white trim. I shivered. Outside this office, blue was my favorite color. I loved drawing oceans and rivers with a blue crayon, and I loved the way the blue in my little brother's eyes grew brighter as we played. But I hated blue walls—especially blue walls with white trim.

The vinyl chair creaked under my weight as I sat down. As hard as I tried, I could not prevent my eyes from searching for the sign just outside the exam room that claimed *Painless Dentist Upstairs*.

"Hello, Christina!" The dentist greeted me when he opened the door, indicating he was ready for me. "It's so nice to see you."

"It's so nice to see you, too," I lied as I climbed into the chair.

"Let me see," he said as he turned on the bright light above my face before digging a sharp instrument into my back tooth. "There it is."

He removed the instrument and dropped it on the tray with a noisy clang. Then he reached for the drill. As the high-pitched screech shrieked through my head, I thought about my conversation with my mother as I was leaving for school that morning.

"But, Mommy, Nadine says she gets Novocain when she has a cavity."

My mother, who had been busy scribbling the note that would release me from class, answered, "Well, you are not Nadine." She folded the note and handed it to me. Then she reached for my little brother, who was clinging to her leg and crying.

"Do you know how the dentist gives you Novocain, Christina?" my older brother asked, allowing no time for me to answer before he continued. "He takes a great big needle, and he *jams* it into your gums."

I winced, then answered, "But Nadine says it doesn't hurt."

"Stop teasing your sister," my mother warned.

"Nadine's a liar," he said.

"How do you know?" I asked, knowing that there was not even one filling in my brother's mouth. I, on the other hand, had a whole mouth full of silver.

My mother's tone had become firm. "Christina, you know your father needs a new tractor, so there is no money for Novocain," she said. "You'll be fine."

But now, as the drill spun closer to the nerve, my heart pounded and I felt as though I were outside of my body, looking down at myself stretched out on the chair with my mouth open, body trembling, and knuckles white struggling against my sadness. Did my parents believe I was worth less than a new tractor?

"I'm sorry, Christina. I'm almost done," the dentist apologized. With a kind hand, he used the white bib that was hanging around my neck to wipe the corner of my mouth. Then he dried a tear that was sliding down my cheek. "I wish I could do this without hurting you," he said in a soothing tone.

"It's okay," I answered. "Daddy needs a new tractor, so we don't have money for Novocain."

Several months later, my mother came into the house with several bags of clothing purchased from a local department store that had suffered damage in a fire. The inventory that had not been ruined had been marked down for clearance. As she proudly pulled the items out one by one, a delighted smile on her face, my father frowned.

"You need to take it all back," he ordered.

Her smile faded.

"But they were so inexpensive, and the kids need them," she protested.

"It doesn't matter. You know I need to buy seeds for spring planting. Take that stuff back."

As my mother returned to the car, heavy bags in her hands, her shoulders were slumped in defeat.

By the time I was seventeen, not much had changed except that it was becoming clearer to me I had more to offer than just my ability to work hard on the farm.

"You've got a real champion here," the vet praised, shaking my father's hand. "She's got all the facts and figures about these animals right there in her head. That's pretty remarkable. I could use someone like her in my office."

My dad smiled and thanked him, but then walked away quickly without saying a word to me. Shortly afterward, though, he offered to teach me how to do the books for his small wholesale electronics company which supplemented the farm income. I was excited when, after a few months, he gave me more responsibility. Although he never said it out loud, I reasoned that I must have been doing a good job if he was giving me more work to do.

One night during my senior year, after handing my dad a reconciled bank statement, I said, "Daddy, Terry asked me to the prom." I wasn't generally allowed to date, but my dad liked Terry, who often drove out to the farm to see me.

"Well, I hope you have a good time," he said with a smile.

My heart was pounding as I prepared myself. Asking for money was nerve-racking for me, but this was my senior prom, and I was hoping for a store-bought dress. "Do you think I could have some money for a dress?" I asked.

The expression on my father's face immediately closed. "Your grandmother sent a box of fabric last week. You can make yourself a dress."

I sighed. Although I was a good seamstress, I didn't believe I could make a dress special enough for an event like the prom. "But, Daddy, I would love to get one from the mall."

Turning away, he asked, "What have you done around here that makes you think you deserve money for a dress?"

I glanced at the reconciled bank statement on the desk. I had been working with him for more than six months without payment, and I was up every morning at five o'clock for both barn and house chores. I had the calluses on my hands to prove it. As much as I wanted to get a job so I could pay for things myself, he wouldn't allow it, because having a job somewhere else would interfere with my responsibilities at home. Plus, on several occasions my dad had said his payment to me was that he provided me with food and shelter.

I took a deep breath to fortify my courage. "Well, I do all my chores around here, plus I'm helping you do the books."

At that, he turned to face me. "You're not making me any money doing bookwork." Pointing out the window to where the animals grazed in the field, he said, "Those cows are making me money. You, on the other hand, are costing me money." A sense of powerlessness ran through me when he said those words, and I fought back the tears that threatened. I knew the cows were making him money, but I was worth something, too, wasn't I?

Feeling defeated, I turned away to hide my tears of frustration and then headed toward the attic where the box of fabric my grandmother had sent was stored. Opening the box, I pulled out the fabrics and ran my fingers over each piece in turn. I found consolation in a soft green satin that would accentuate the green in my eyes.

Several weeks later, my friend Cindy called, asking if I would help her pick out her prom dress. On the appointed day, we wandered from store to store with her mom, Rose. In each store, the two of us watched Cindy try on dresses and pick out accessories to match. Cindy was tall and willowy, and she looked stunning in almost everything she tried on.

"Christina, why don't you try on this one?" Rose asked, holding up a pretty pink dress. The color was so delicate, and the fabric draped in soft folds over her arm.

I had no money to buy it, but I carried it to the dressing room anyway. Pulling it over my head, I prayed that it would look awful, but as it fell over my shoulders and then swished over my body, I thought, *Darn. It's perfect.* Standing in front of the mirror, I felt the familiar rush of frustration when I thought about how hard I worked, and still I had no means to purchase a store-bought dress like the ones my friends would be wearing.

When I swirled in front of Cindy and her mom, I was beaming.

"I knew it would be beautiful on you, Christina!" Rose smiled.

"You need to get it!" Cindy encouraged me, adding, "Terry will love you in it!"

I smiled, shaking my head, and then returned to the dressing room. Placing the dress back on the hanger with a sigh, I ran my fingers over the fabric one more time. It was so beautiful.

Later, when we stopped for a late lunch, I studied the menu as

Cindy and Rose placed their orders. When the waitress turned to take my order, I said, "Nothing for me, thank you."

Rose looked concerned. "But we've been shopping all day, Christina. You need to eat something."

"I'll eat when I get home," I answered with a smile.

Rose's eyebrows knitted, and she frowned. "Did your parents send you shopping with no money?"

"I'm not really shopping," I said defensively. "I'm just looking."

She and Cindy exchanged a quick glance. "But you are working for your dad," Rose pressed. She had mentioned earlier that my dad had bragged about what a great job I was doing for him.

"Yes," I answered. "It's a lot of fun."

Now her face darkened, and she looked confused. "Well, isn't he paying you?"

Embarrassed, I felt my face flush pink. I admired Rose. She often told me that I was a talented young woman, and I didn't want her to see me as just a silly kid. To make it worse, I was embarrassed that she might see my father as taking advantage of me.

By then I knew that Rose didn't have a very high opinion of my parents, so I rushed to defend my dad. "There's no money to pay me, and that's okay. Cindy must have told you that we're building a new barn, right? Besides, I'm enjoying it because I'm learning so much about business."

Once more she and Cindy exchanged a look, and this time when the waitress returned, Rose said, "Please bring her a tuna salad sandwich and a cup of tea."

"That's not necessary," I whispered.

"You need to eat," she insisted. "Besides," she added, "you work so hard, and you're such a good kid. You should be paid for the work you do."

In the end, I decided not to go to the prom. As nice as the dress that I had made was, it just didn't feel special enough. But more than that, I was beginning to feel a great sense of sadness that, no matter how hard I worked, in my parents' eyes I would always be worth less. I was just like that homemade prom dress hanging unworn in my closet: not special or good enough.

By the time I was ready for college, I was grateful that I was accustomed to working hard, because with only a small grant to help me out, I would need to work my way through school. The anxiety I had felt as a kid was now a constant knot in my stomach as I endlessly worried I wouldn't have enough money to finish my studies.

Soon after starting my freshman year, I borrowed a typewriter and started a business, typing term papers.

I was determined to make it on my own.

Years later, with college well behind me and a baby in my near future, I took a part-time job close to my house.

"I can only pay you minimum wage," my prospective boss apologized. "We're a start-up company, so money is tight."

"That's okay," I answered with enthusiasm. "Being on the ground floor of a start-up business is a great opportunity."

As months and then years went by, the company grew quickly, and I was given more and more responsibility. Although I received a raise each year, very quickly the raises were not reflective of the type or amount of work that was expected of me. Colleagues in comparative positions were boasting of salaries that were substantially higher than mine, so with this in mind, one afternoon I knocked on my boss's open office door.

"Can we talk?"

He looked up from his computer with a welcoming grin. "Sure, Chrissie. Come on in."

Prior to this meeting he and I had had several informal conversations about increasing my rate of pay, so I was confused when he asked, "Why do you think you deserve more money?"

Hiding my frustration, I once more listed my past and current accomplishments, noting several awards and recognitions I had received in my field, as well as the community service I did in the name of the company.

He nodded his head as I spoke, seemingly in agreement. I was stunned, therefore, when his response brought me back to that discussion with my dad nearly twenty years earlier. With a frown, he said, "I know you work hard, Chrissie, and I appreciate that. But let's face it—you're not making me any money." My heart pounded and my knees felt weak when he added, "The salespeople are making me money. You and the whole accounting department are just costing me money."

As I slowly walked down the hallway, I felt defeated and completely powerless. The determination and drive that had sustained me for years was wavering. Climbing the stairs to my office, I had a disheartening thought: *Maybe it's true. Maybe I really am worth less . . .*

Discovery

Growing up, I learned that love is conditional. It was only earned through hard work, and even then the standards were seemingly impossible to meet. Even when I met or exceeded my parents' standards, praise was rarely given. As a result, I developed a thirst for approval that fueled me to take on more and more responsibility and work harder for smaller rewards—thus setting up an unhealthy pattern that extended into all other areas in my life. Right through adulthood, I allowed myself to be undervalued in both my personal and professional lives.

I now understand that children need to feel unconditional love, acceptance, and understanding in order to know their own worth. Without a sense of worth, negative self-talk can become an unhealthy pattern, leading to feeling "not good enough" well into adulthood.

At a very early age, I understood the concept of a balance sheet. I learned that an asset is valuable, something that provides income. The cows were assets because their milk provided my parents money, which bought food and clothing for the family. A liability, on the other hand, is something that works to a person's disadvantage, such as a payment due to another person or an institution. I learned that I was a liability because by my very existence I was costing my parents money, and it seemed to me they did not feel I was adding any value. To make matters worse, I was often sick and needed additional medical and dental care, which cost extra money.

Because my parents felt that farm expenses were more important than the cost of Novocain, I was exposed to the trauma of undergoing painful dental procedures without the aid of appropriate medication. Compounding the trauma was the fact that my parents did not accompany me to the appointments to offer support and comfort.

I learned to cope with these terrifying dental procedures and other similar situations by dissociating (disconnecting) from my body. Dissociating is the body's fail-safe mechanism when stress and anxiety levels become too severe. Until recently, I continued to disconnect from my body on a regular basis to avoid feeling physical or emotional pain and the negative thoughts associated with it. I no longer detach in negative situations because I now understand that when I am disconnected, I am unable to discern when my personal boundaries are being crossed—and maybe more importantly, I am not fully present in my life.

For where your treasure is, there will your heart be also.

—LUKE 12:34 (ESV)

Pink Bubble Gum Snow Cone

I was bored out of my mind. The late spring sun slanted in through the windows as a shirtless jogger sprinted past. With only a few weeks left until the end of my freshman year of college, the weather had finally warmed up enough—at least for one day—to remove our heavy coats. With the heat still cranked high, the lecture hall was warm. To make matters worse, I was wearing heavy jeans with a long-sleeved, black plaid blouse. As the professor droned on, sweat ran down between my breasts, dampening my waistband. I looked at the clock. Twenty more minutes.

My eyes wandered the room, studying the other students. Some looked out the windows; others doodled in the margins of their notebooks. This was a required class, and we had been held prisoner for thirteen weeks now by a professor who was completely devoid of any creativity when it came to the presentation of the material. *Just add water*, I thought.

On the windowsill, a black fly buzzed, spinning on its back, dying a slow death in a frantic dance. When it fell to the floor, the buzzing abruptly ended under the sole of the sandal worn by a classmate in a pair of tight blue jeans and a short shirt. I had seen her before, of course, but I did not know her. Now, though, I was completely captivated as she scraped the oozing carcass off the bottom of her shoe. The frothy white blouse not quite covering her torso was sleeveless and wide open in the front. Her breasts, held in by only a slip of a bra, threatened to spill out as she bent forward. I envied her outfit, but, more, I envied the ease with which she wore it. Then I glanced at my own outfit, one that was finished off with a pair of thick-soled army boots. *If I looked like her, I would dress like that*, I thought.

I studied her for a full thirty seconds, noting her astounding cheekbones, small nose, and long fingers. Her thick, dark hair hung in tendrils around her pink cheeks, and the smooth tan that covered her arms hinted at a trip to someplace warm during spring break—or at the very least a twice-weekly visit to the nearby tanning salon. I found some pleasure in noting the rather ample belly that protruded over the jeans that were slung low across her hips. The bulging flesh resembled a pink bubble gum snow cone, the kind that was sold at the annual county fair. *Ha!* I thought to myself. *Not so perfect after all.*

That protruding belly held a certain fascination for me as my own mother's voice echoed in my mind, on a loop since childhood.

"Pull in your stomach, young lady."

Each time I heard those words, I would suck my belly in as close to my backbone as possible, wishing it would just stay there without such constant effort. I would often press my hand against my stomach and think, *There has to be a better way* . . .

"Maybe a girdle would help," my mother had suggested one morning as I hurried out the door for middle school.

Reaching down now, my fingers touched the mound lying just above my own lap. It was full and hung over the wide macramé belt that was the style of the time. "The freshman fifteen," my brother had commented one day as he poked at it.

Exploring further, my hands ran over the side where more flesh hung. I desperately searched in vain for something solid, but all I found was more thick mush. Suddenly I looked down in horror, all thoughts of the boring lecture gone. When had my belly gotten so big?

When class ended, I rushed across campus and back to my dorm room. Throwing the door open, I announced, "Judy, I need your help."

My roommate's face lit up with laughter as I related the story of the boring lecture and the pink bubble gum snow cone.

"You're crazy," she said with a laugh, tossing her brown hair over her shoulder and closing the book on her lap.

"No, I'm not," I insisted. "I need your help. I need to start doing sit-ups. Right now." I kicked off my boots. "Please—all you have to do is hold my feet." She put her book down on the bed as she unfolded her legs and stood up.

As I pulled off my socks, I made a face. "Phew," I said, rushing to the bathroom to wash my smelly feet. Towel in hand, I hurried back to our room where my roommate now sat on the floor, waiting.

Sitting down in front of her, I tucked the towel under the base of my spine and pulled up my knees.

"Really, Chrissie, you are certifiable," she said, giggling as she moved onto her knees to grab hold of my ankles.

I thought it would be easy. Wiggling my shoulders, I folded my fingers together and tucked them behind my head. With a grunt, I pulled my body upward, imagining I was holding the same perfect form of the toned girls I had seen in the gym. Instead, there I was, in the exact same spot, looking at Judy's grinning face just over the top of my knees.

Once more, I gave it my best effort, grateful for the pressure of Judy's hands on my ankles as I strained forward. *This is embarrassing.* Letting out another effortful grunt, louder this time, I couldn't believe it when I didn't move even an inch.

"How about not locking your hands behind your head?" Judy suggested.

"Where should I put them?" I asked.

She considered my question, shaking her head in concentration, and said, "How about you put them on your shoulders or right out in front of you?"

Mustering all the strength I had, with my arms parallel to my legs, I gave another giant heave—one accompanied by an even louder groan.

Judy cheered when I came up off the floor, my face red from the effort.

"Yay! You did it! Now do another one!"

Sweat ran down from my armpits as I tried again. This time, though, I was unsuccessful.

"I'll try again tomorrow," I promised.

As the days went by, I got stronger. I was encouraged when each day I was able to add another sit-up. By the time the semester ended three weeks later, I congratulated myself that I was up to almost twenty-five.

"You look good," said Jerry, my on-again, off-again boyfriend, when we met on the day he returned from college. "What have you been doing?"

As he sipped his coffee, I shared the story of the pink bubble gum snow cone and my smelly feet.

"Whatever it takes for motivation," he said, laughing.

Growing up, I was a fat kid. I don't remember the first time I heard it, but I think it was before I knew how to walk. "She's so chubby! Look at that little belly!"

Being chubby with a little belly is cute until you're about seven. After that it's just discouraging.

"She's not fat," my grandmother scolded my mom one summer afternoon as they sat chatting at the kitchen table. "She's pleasingly plump."

Thanks, Grandma, I thought. *That makes me feel so much better.*

"Don't eat that!" my mother would caution when I licked the remaining cookie batter out of the bowl. She often put me on diets in which a meal was restricted to small plates of canned peaches set on a bed of lettuce and then topped with a dollop of cottage cheese.

"But, Mommy, I really want a piece of cake," I'd whimper.

"You don't need it," she'd insist. "You're already too heavy."

I'd drop my head, trying to hide the tears of frustration and embarrassment as my family downed their big slices of cake with thick frosting.

What my mother didn't know was that while she was feeding the baby or talking with my sister in the living room or burning the garbage in the backyard, I was grabbing a napkin, quickly cutting off a slab of cake, hungrily licking the knife, and then dashing upstairs to my bedroom. Opening the closet door, I would climb inside and then, by the light coming in through a knothole, I'd savor the sweet treat. When I was finished, I'd hide the telltale napkin deep in the bathroom garbage can where I knew no one would see it.

Often, during certain periods of restriction, I would dig through the bins of cow grain, searching for the thick balls of molasses which I would stuff into my mouth when no one was looking, washing them down with water from the faucet in the milk house. I was convinced that I was a hopeless case.

Years later, after my second son, Benjamin, was born, I needed clothes for work, so I took both boys shopping with me. In the dressing room, as my son Christofer watched me pull on a pair of dress pants, he studied my post-baby body with a look of disgust. Pointing to my stretched and sagging belly and then to his little brother sitting in the carrier on the floor, he wrinkled his nose and said accusingly, "*He* did that to you."

Because I had injured my back while delivering Benjamin, I wasn't able to do sit-ups for a while. So, the very next day, I drove to the local YWCA to begin swimming.

As the years went by nothing had really changed. Each time I passed a mirror, I inspected my body. The first thing I would do was suck in my belly as hard as I could. Once I was satisfied that I had pulled it in as far as it would go, I'd make a note of the excess bulge poking out above and below my bra line. Next, I would pinch the small spare tire that is a family trait, checking to be sure it wasn't a full inch. Last, I would flex the muscles in my thighs, noting where they were still flabby. Everywhere I went, I couldn't help but focus on the long, slender waists, even longer legs, and flat tummies of the women around me. I couldn't help wondering why I had never looked like that.

I was right around fifty years old when a conversation with

my friend Jewel gave me a new perspective on my body type.

As we attempted to talk on the phone early one morning, every few minutes her two young girls interrupted. Finally, as she began to run out of patience, she said, "Marie, honey, don't pull the cat's tail. You'll hurt her. Angelina, will you please go wash your sister's hands?"

There was a bit of a scuffle, and then I heard Angelina whine, "But, Mom!"

"Honey, I'm talking to Chrissie. Please just wash your sister's hands."

I couldn't help smiling when I heard her exasperated sigh. "Okay, Mom."

When it grew quiet, Jewel dropped her voice to a low whisper. "I've been worried about Angelina," she admitted.

"Why?" I asked. Jewel's daughter Angelina was a beautiful honey blonde with the most interesting eyes framed by thick, dark lashes.

Jewel's next words hit me right in my protruding little belly.

"I've been a little worried about her weight."

Hearing her say those words was like listening in on conversations between my mother and grandmother many years earlier. For a moment, I was my seven-year-old self, cut to the quick as they discussed the problem that weighed heavier on my shoulders than a huge chocolate cake covered in chocolate frosting and a generous coating of rainbow sprinkles.

I felt instant compassion for this beautiful little girl. But more than that, I worried she might overhear our conversation and then carry a bad body image around with her for many years, the same way I had. Even as an adult, whenever I looked in the mirror, I still saw the word *fat* emblazoned in neon, like a billboard held in front of my oversized figure, blasting out the message just in case anyone had missed it. *Chrissie is fat!* I wanted better for this little girl. I wanted her to *know* that, no matter what, she was beautiful. I needed her to *feel* she was beautiful, and I wanted her to *live* as beautiful.

All these thoughts ran through my head in a banana-split second. But my fears were dispelled with Jewel's next words. "But I realized the other day that there's nothing to worry about at all. She's just built like you."

Quite honestly, I had no idea what she meant. If Angelina was built like me, she must be pleasingly plump, chubby, or at the very least big-boned. She must have a belly she could never suck in tight enough, and she must have a spare tire around her waist.

Then Jewel explained. "Angelina is muscular. She's strong. Just like you."

In that moment, I realized what a lucky girl Angelina was to have Jewel as her mother. *Strong,* I thought as I carried the phone to the mirror in the bedroom, where I could examine my body from a new perspective. I pulled up my shirt to expose the pure white skin beneath. Turning right and then left, I studied the thick line that pulled in just under my rib cage. Then I examined the round muscles covering my shoulders, flexing them first up and then down. I twisted my body back and forth, raising my arms. The muscles were not stereotypically feminine, but they were thick and strong.

As I studied my legs, the words of a high-school friend ran through my mind. "Hey, we need a ride. Let's have Chrissie stick out a leg and trip a car!" My friend had been teasing, of course, but he had also been right. The legs that had carried me through life *were* strong.

For a moment, I thought about what I had been doing. By soaking in the words of those around me, I had been merciless toward myself. Not only had I taken their words *in*, I had taken them *on*, wearing them like a badge and shrinking under their weight. *Fat. Big-boned. Big girl.*

I want better for myself, I thought as I studied my reflection. Tossing my hair back, I stood a little straighter and smiled. *From now on, I am going to live beautiful, because I* am *beautiful.*

Discovery

My battle with a bad body image started when I was a small child. Being referred to as "fat" was hurtful, damaging to my self-esteem, and the cause of a lifetime of food issues. By the time I was in middle school, "fat" had become part of my identity. This label did not motivate me to lose weight, which I'm sure was my mother's intention. Instead, it caused me to become a closet eater. Because of this label, I was not only ashamed of my body; I was ashamed of my love of food.

I now understand that it is my body *type* (short, muscular, and compact) that did not meet my mother's perception of beauty. She worried that others might view me the same way she did and that I might be a poor reflection on her. She was so concerned about not having the "perfect daughter" that she was incapable of seeing the special beauty that was mine.

It wasn't until I was fifty years old that I realized I saw only specific parts of my body as fat and, therefore, ugly. It had been my habit to focus on those "bad" parts rather than to see my body as a whole entity. It took me many years to undo the damage that was caused by others' destructive comments, but I am now able to see myself as a whole, healthy, and beautiful person.

The words of the reckless pierce like swords,
but the tongue of the wise brings healing.

—PROVERBS 12:18 (NIV)

The First No

I cringed with shame every time I thought about it. The entire thing had been my fault, and maybe I deserved the guilt that ate at me every single minute of every single day.

I was nineteen when it happened. At that point in my life, I was a hardworking college student who didn't have a lot of time for fun. That night, though, I had decided to go out for a drink with my girlfriends. I had one, then another, and then a third as we danced and sang. It was the Saturday before the beginning of finals, and we were having a great time, blowing off some steam.

"Hey, that guy over there is checking you out," said my room-mate, Kathy, pointing to a handsome blond who waved at me from across the room.

I laughed, by then just a bit tipsy.

"He's not checking me out. That's my friend Schuyler. He's engaged."

When I smiled back at him, he moved in our direction.

"Hi, handsome," my friend Diane said flirtatiously.

I shook my head and giggled. "Don't pay any attention to her. She flirts with everybody."

He glanced at Diane and then turned to me. "I'm surprised to see you out," he said. "I thought you'd be studying for exams."

I was feeling happier and much lighter than I had in a long time. Exams started on Monday, but I was prepared. Besides, I was a straight-A student, so I wasn't worried.

"Doesn't a girl get to have a little fun once in a while?"

"Sure, most girls get out and have fun all the time. I'm just surprised to see *you* out," he answered.

As the band once more began to play, I swayed to the beat, closing my eyes and floating on an alcohol-induced buzz.

"Do you want to dance?" he asked.

"Sure!" I agreed.

We strolled out onto the middle of the dance floor where he took my hand and then spun me around. "Hey, you really know how to dance!" I said with admiration.

"I know how to do a lot of things," he said, his beautiful eyes lighting up with a smile.

I had never noticed the stunning blue of his eyes, the thick muscles in his arms, or how tall and sexy he was when he walked. *Must be the drinks*, I thought.

I had met Schuyler about eighteen months earlier, during the first week of my freshman year. He was a local guy, living at home with his family and commuting to campus for classes. We had been paired up in archaeology class, and then he chose me for his partner in psychology. When the professor nodded his head in agreement to Schuyler picking me as a partner, Schuyler said, "Thanks, Professor." A few of our classmates laughed when he added, "She studies."

Schuyler and I often found ourselves in casual conversations after class, and those conversations usually ended up with a cup of coffee in the campus café. He frequently talked about his long-term girlfriend, Stephanie, to whom he was now engaged. She had been awarded a scholarship from a college in Vermont, where she was majoring in theater and minoring in business.

"She wants to make sure she has a backup plan, just in case the whole theater thing doesn't work out."

"Smart girl," I had answered.

He nodded his head and smiled. "She sure is. I'm a lucky guy."

After dancing for a while, he asked, "Do you want another drink?"

Wiping the sweat off my brow, I accepted.

He bought two rum and Cokes that he placed on the table in front of an empty seat, signaling me over.

I pointed to my girlfriends, indicating that I was hanging out with them, but he walked over to grab my hand and pulled me toward the table. "Sit with me?" he asked.

I shrugged at my girlfriends, who were looking in my direction as he escorted me away. I laughed when Diane gave me a thumbs-up.

I sipped the sweet drink, my body continuing to move to the music even as I sat at the table. It had been some time since I had felt so at ease. The semester had been stressful. Carrying twenty-one credits while working twenty-five hours a week had turned out to be much more difficult than I had anticipated. Long days turned into long nights of studying, especially since I continued to sing in both the select choir and the campus chorus.

As the night progressed, Schuyler and I danced some more, we had one more drink, and when the band announced that their last song would be a popular ballad, he asked, "Dance with me?"

"I don't think Stephanie would like it if she saw us slow-dancing," I answered, moving away.

He laughed. "She doesn't care. She knows you and I are good friends."

I smiled and then changed my mind, stepping into his arms. Swaying along to the music, I closed my eyes, laid my cheek on his chest, and began quietly singing along.

"I love when you sing, Chrissie."

"You do?" I asked, surprised, raising my head to look into his eyes. "When have you heard me sing?"

"Sometimes when you're practicing with the select choir, I sit in the back of the rehearsal hall."

"You do?"

He nodded his head. "It's right across from the commuter student lounge."

I nodded and then once more placed my head on his chest.

"When you sing," he added, "it sounds so beautiful."

I was flattered. "Well, if you like music, you should join the campus chorus," I offered. "We need male voices."

He shrugged and shook his head. "That would be great except that I can't carry a tune in a bucket."

When the music ended, Diane signaled me over, so I hurried away to where my friends were gathering their coats. "We're going to head back to the dorm. Are you coming with us?"

Grabbing my coat from the chair, I answered, "Yes. I need to get some sleep."

But then Schuyler came up behind me and touched my shoulder. "I'm hungry. Do you think maybe you'd want to go to Justine's with me? They make a really good omelet there."

I glanced between him and my friends, feeling torn. I had intended to spend the evening with them and was already feeling a bit bad that I had been ignoring them. But I considered his offer anyway. "You guys don't mind?" I asked.

They shook their heads, and Diane winked. "Go," she encouraged.

"I'm buying!" Schuyler offered, his tone persuasive.

"Well, I *am* hungry," I admitted.

"Great!" He turned to my girlfriends to add, "I'll drop her off at the dorm afterwards."

When I finished a three-egg omelet with toast and bacon he commented, "You've got an impressive appetite."

"No one has ever accused me of skimping on meals," I answered, pointing to my thighs. Sipping the last of my tea, I said, "Tonight really was fun. Thank you, Schuyler. And thank you for a very late dinner—or maybe it's a very early breakfast."

Pulling on his coat and jingling his keys, he said, "You're welcome. I had a lot of fun, too, but now, I need to get you home."

He helped me into my coat and then held the door for me.

Only minutes later, we arrived at my dorm, where most of the windows were dark.

"It's late. You don't need to walk me to the door," I protested when he stepped out of the car.

"That's exactly *why* I'm going to walk with you," he said.

He's so nice. Stephanie sure is a lucky girl, I thought with a twinge of envy.

Unlocking the heavy front door, I pushed it open and let myself in.

"Good night, Schuyler," I said.

He followed me into the lobby. "I want to be sure you get to your room safely," he insisted.

I lived in an all-girl dorm, and men weren't allowed in the building at that time of night. Normally, I was not a rule breaker, but I knew he was just making sure I was safe, so I agreed.

When we got upstairs he asked, "Can I see your room?"

"Sure, but then you really have to go. I don't want to get in trouble for having a guy on the floor."

"You won't," he answered confidently.

I slid the key into the lock and then pushed the door open.

"Nice," he said, looking around the room. "No roommate?"

"She's away for the weekend," I answered. "It's her boy-friend's birthday."

"Her boyfriend's birthday? I wonder what they're doing right now," he said.

The suggestive tone of his voice made me uncomfortable.

"I'm sure they're sleeping," I answered, suddenly feeling the need to check the space between him and the door to the hallway. When I noticed he was blocking it, I said, "Okay, well, you've seen my room, so you really should go."

He smiled and stepped closer. Then he drew me toward him, lifted my chin, and kissed me. My eyes flew open in surprise, but then I relaxed into the kiss. *What am I doing?* I thought. *What about Stephanie?* The kiss was lingering, and I floated on the sensation as he walked me slowly backward to my small bed.

"Schuyler, what are you doing?" I asked.

Again, he kissed me, this time pushing me down onto the bed. Suddenly he yanked at the top of my jeans, snapping me back to reality.

"Schuyler? What are you *doing?*"

"What do you think I'm doing?" he asked.

He shoved his full weight on top of me. I pushed at him, trying to get him off me. "Schuyler! No!"

As he forced my jeans farther down, restraining me with one hand, he accused, "You've been flirting with me all night long."

My mind ran crazy trying to figure out how anything that had occurred between us could have been misunderstood as flirting.

"I have not!" I said. I knew my voice was bordering somewhere between angry and scared.

With a wry grin, he ripped at my panties, which immediately tore. When the chill of the room hit my exposed bottom, I was completely mortified, but the feeling instantly turned to fear. *This can't be happening.*

"Schuyler, *no!*" Once more, I struggled against him with every bit of strength I had left, but then he violently thrust into me, causing a searing pain to shoot through my entire lower body.

I don't recall what happened after that or how long it went on. It's as though I left my body, coming back when he headed to the door to leave. With his hand on the doorknob he turned back toward me.

"I didn't know you were a virgin, Chrissie," he said, his voice low.

As I stood in the shower, letting the hot, soapy water run over my body, I promised myself I would never tell anyone what had happened. I shouldn't have been drinking. I shouldn't have gone to eat with someone else's fiancée. I should never have let him into my room. I should not have let him kiss me, and I definitely should not have kissed him back. The whole thing was all my fault.

I dreaded Monday morning when I would see him in the classroom where I would take my first exam. But he barely glanced in my direction. Instead, he bent his head over his paper, finished quickly, and left.

The following semester he was in two of my classes, each time choosing a different partner when pairing up was required. Sometimes I would find myself staring at the back of his head, willing him to turn around.

But he never did.

Two years later, I sat curled up with a book on my lap while my friends got ready to go out.

"Chrissie, why are you such a stick in the mud? I wish you'd go out with us," Chloe coaxed.

"No," I answered. "I have to be at work early tomorrow."

"That's what you always say," she said, looking a little hurt. I shrugged and turned my eyes back to the book.

As they readied to leave, once more she pressed. "You should come. Ronnie's going to be there, and you know he really likes you."

Again, I shook my head. "Not interested."

Suddenly, out of the blue, she blurted out, "Are you a lesbian?"

I burst out laughing so hard that when I threw my head back, I knocked it into the wall behind me. Still giggling and rubbing my head, I responded, "No, I'm not a lesbian. I'm just not interested in a stupid football player who has no foreseeable future beyond graduation."

Her response was quick. "You know very well he's got a double major in international business and economics. I believe he'll be going somewhere beyond the football field with those credentials."

Of course, I knew all that. Ronnie and I were in several classes together and often had dinner at the long, crowded table in the cafeteria. I was comfortable with him. But I had been comfortable with Schuyler, too.

"Seriously, girls, I don't want to date. I've got too much to do."

Listening to their laughter slowly fading away as they headed down the hallway, my eyes misted over. Sighing, I laid the book on my bed and looked out the window at the stars twinkling in a pitch-black sky. I would love to date Ronnie. He was beautiful:

nearly six-foot-four, with dark hair and hazel eyes. Plus, he seemed nice—but therein lay the problem. I hadn't spent any time alone with him, and I had made up my mind that I wouldn't. I didn't want to find out I was wrong . . . again.

A few weeks later, Chloe returned unexpectedly from the St. Patrick's Day party that was going on down the hall.

"Chrissie, I wish you'd come. We're having such a good time, and Ronnie's there." She added, "He's asking for you."

I shook my head. "No, Chloe. I can't."

"Why?" she insisted. "You're such a nice person, but you shut yourself away in here. You can't just study and work all the time. You need to have some fun."

"I *can't*," I insisted.

Now she pressed. "Why?"

The onslaught of hot, raging tears came out of nowhere. Sobs wracked my body as Chloe stood in shocked surprise. "What's the matter?" she asked. I cried even harder when she coaxed, "Please, Chrissie, I want to help you."

Finally, the story poured out. I told her everything—the drinking, the dancing, the three-egg omelet, me allowing him into the room, the unexpected kiss, and him forcing himself on me. Then I told her about the crying in the shower and my guilt and shame as the blood and semen trickled down my leg, running in a thin red line toward the drain. It was such a relief to finally tell someone about it.

"It was all my fault," I sniffled once the sobs had subsided.

But Chloe was adamant.

"No, it wasn't your fault," she insisted. "It was *his* fault. You told him to stop. And he didn't."

I shook my head, so she placed her hands on my shoulders, her eyes drilling into mine. "It was *his* fault, Chrissie. Are you hearing what I'm telling you? It was *not* your fault."

As I looked deep into her kind eyes, I wanted to believe her. "Don't tell anyone," I begged.

She nodded, promising to keep my secret safe.

"You really should talk to a counselor, though," she suggested. "This isn't something you should keep to yourself."

But I didn't want to talk to anyone. I didn't want anyone to know how stupid I had been.

Several years later, while I was riding in the car with my mother, every hair on my arms stood at attention as she talked.

"Some college girl is accusing a boy of raping her," she said, her disapproving tone freezing a spot in the center of my stomach. "It's ridiculous. These girls come on to the boys, and then, when the boys take them up on it, they're calling it rape."

Her words catapulted me back to the moment when I'd violently lost my virginity to a guy I thought was my friend. I wished, for just a moment, that she could see that young girl through my experience.

"That boy's reputation will be wrecked because of her. It's shameful."

I felt like a deer caught in the headlights of an oncoming car, paralyzed and unable to react as I willed myself to finally break my silence.

My heart was pounding hard in my chest when I said, "But, Mom, maybe he *did* rape her. Maybe it wasn't her fault."

My mother sniffed, fueled by her opinion and maybe her ignorance. I refused to believe it was from her lack of compassion.

"Young girls these days are little sluts, and they get what they deserve. I'm sure she was strutting around half-dressed, just asking for it."

"I didn't get what I deserved when it happened to me."

For a moment she was silent, and then she asked, "What are you saying?"

I let the words hang between us without explanation for several more moments, giving her time to absorb the significance of my admission. Her tone was accusing when she finally asked, "Why didn't you say anything?"

This time I snapped back.

"Because if I *had* said something—if I was as brave as this girl is—everyone would have been talking about me the same way you're talking about her."

She did not look in my direction.

We drove in silence for several minutes before she flicked off the radio and once again broke my heart.

"Let's talk about something happier," she said.

Discovery

Being raped by a guy I thought was my friend was traumatic on many levels. The physical effects were obvious, but the psychological damage took me years to overcome. For years I replayed the events in my head. I couldn't stop blaming myself because I believed that I had inadvertently caused it.

After that incident, I was fearful around men because I no longer trusted myself to be able to accurately discern their character or sense their motives. I protected myself the only way I knew how, which was to immerse myself in my work and studies. I was careful never to be alone with a man for several years afterward. Along with the rape went any shreds of safety I had left. It was difficult to come to terms with the fact that he had robbed me of my virginity, something I had valued and wanted to give to a man I loved.

Until now, only a small handful of people knew about this incident. I've shared it here only because it is my hope that my story will help others who have experienced this type of dehumanizing trauma. Suffering through this ordeal has led me to fully understand the heartbreaking stigma of rape, which is made worse by the number of people who continue to blame the victim. Rape is never predictable; the rapist may be someone you know and even consider a friend, or he could even have the demeanor of gentleman. Alcohol use is never an excuse for someone to cross your personal boundaries. Rape begins at the *first no*.

For whenever our heart condemns us,
God is greater than our heart, and he knows everything.

—1 John 3:20 (ESV

Part Two

Chocolate and Carrot Soup

"She really likes you," Carlene said with a smile as Bella, the German shepherd that Carlene had inherited when she met her husband, laid her head on my lap.

"What's not to like?" I asked as I gently rubbed the soft spot on Bella's ear. Then I giggled. "She doesn't care that I talk too much, my teeth are crooked, and I'm a big loser!"

By then Carlene and I had been working on the stories for this book for almost six months, and we hadn't lost our sense of humor about all that I shared.

But as the laughter died away, a sudden feeling of nostalgia caused my eyes to mist.

"I can't believe you're moving out of here," I said as I looked around the room. The huge plants that had softened the corners for the last seven years had already been moved to her new husband's house, and there were cardboard boxes piled one inside of the other on the table waiting to be filled with kitchen utensils and the small prints that still hung on the wall.

She sighed as she, too, glanced around that room that now had a hollow sound. "I'm really going to miss this place," Carlene said.

"I'll miss it, too," I said. "But I love John, and I'm so happy for you. He's a good man."

She nodded, her brown eyes soft as a smile lit her face. "He really is."

For a moment we sat in silence, the old refrigerator humming in the background, each of us lost in our separate thoughts.

When Carlene unfolded herself from the couch and dropped a handful of drafted stories onto the coffee table, she asked, "Do you want some iced tea?"

The room had grown warm as the sun blasted through the now uncovered living room windows, and I was thirsty. "Absolutely," I answered.

Gently moving Bella's head from my lap, I pushed myself up off the floor where I preferred to sit while we worked.

"Wow, this must be some kind of a record. We've been working for almost three hours, and you haven't gotten into the chocolate yet."

"Oh, don't worry about that. I'm on it," she said, opening the cabinet over the stove and unfolding a bag of chocolate morsels. Popping one into her mouth, she extended the bag and asked, "Want some?"

"No, thanks," I answered as I sat back down on the floor. "I wouldn't want to deprive you of your goodies."

Munching on chocolate and carrying her glass, Carlene wandered back to the couch and once more stretched out her legs. I opened my laptop and glanced at the notes scattered across the floor. "Are you ready to get back to work?" I asked.

"Almost," she said. It was her turn to be thoughtful. Folding her hands as if in prayer, she said, "I was just thinking about how far we've come together."

I nodded, hit by a wave of love for her, the strength of which often astounded me. For it was my relationship with this woman that had played an important role in changing me in the most profound way imaginable.

Ten years earlier, only days after my younger son had left for college, my then-husband, Gabriel, and I had moved to a house in the country that needed significant renovations. Between the mess of the construction and my extremely busy and exhausting job, I was desperate to find a way to relax.

One evening as I flipped through the mail on the kitchen table, I broke the seal on a flyer that announced the schedule of continuing education classes at the local school. A week later, I entered the high school library with my yoga mat, a bottle of water, and the hope of finding a friend.

Minutes before the class started, a tall, attractive brunette bounced in, scanning the room for an available space. I smiled, moved my mat, and pointed to a spot next to me.

"Thanks," she whispered as she settled onto the floor next to me.

Later, as we walked together to the parking lot after class, she introduced herself as Carlene and shared that she, too, was new to the area and looking to make some local friends.

We quickly became friendly, meeting at the local gym for classes or spending evenings taking long walks around a nearby lake. Although I liked her, I remained cautious. It was my pattern never to fully trust women, and not to let any *one* woman know too much about me. As time went by, though, I began to understand that she placed the same importance on the confidences entrusted to her that I did, and that she, too, didn't take friendship lightly. With this dawning realization, I opened up and began sharing things that I had previously kept to myself. It was nearly two years before I fully appreciated that this was a woman I could truly call my friend.

At the time, I was grappling with my emotions over my breakup with my husband, Gabriel, and my health was faltering. Unusual symptoms plagued my body, but test after test came back inconclusive. When the doctor ordered a scan of both my brain and my cervical spine—a procedure that needed to be done the very next day—I called Carlene to let her know I wouldn't be meeting her at the gym that night.

"Are you all right?" she asked.

"Honestly?" I responded, trying desperately to hold my fragile emotions in check. As I clutched the phone tightly in my hand, though, I suddenly began to sob.

"I'll be right over . . . and I'm bringing wine!" she said.

That night, we sat huddled at my kitchen table scribbling a list of questions for the neurologist I would see after my tests.

The following day, while I was being scanned by huge machines and prodded by curious health-care professionals, Carlene sat reading in the waiting room.

"You have no idea how grateful I am," I said as we later stood at the elevator that would take us to the top of the multilevel parking garage.

"I wouldn't want you to go through this all alone," she said. "And I know you would do the same for me."

Only four short months later, her marriage dissolved, and it wasn't long before she and I became each other's support system.

"You're getting too thin," I commented one evening as we walked up the steep hill by my house.

"I am?" she asked, looking down at her body and then back at me.

"Yes," I said. "Your jeans are hanging off your butt, and your cheekbones are sticking right out of your skin."

She hitched up her jeans, then looked over her shoulder as if to verify my observation about her butt.

Laughing, I admitted, "You know I'm jealous, right? I just don't think it's fair that you *lose* weight when you get stressed out."

Truthfully, neither of us was eating well, so that night as we chatted, we resolved that every Wednesday one of us would make a healthy dinner to share with the other.

On one such Wednesday not long afterward, Carlene hung her purse on the back of my kitchen chair and said, "Mmm . . . something smells great!"

As she greeted my dog, Hannah, and then bent down to pet my cat, Trix, I said, "I hope so. I'm trying two new recipes." Pointing to a pan of brownies cooling on the counter, I said, "Gluten-free."

"They smell delicious," she said, sniffing the contents of the pan. Pulling a plate from the cabinet and searching for a knife in the drawer, she asked, "Can I have one now?"

"No," I answered, laughing. "We're supposed to be eating healthy! Didn't your mother ever tell you that dessert comes *after* dinner?"

As she snacked on a brownie, I prepared cucumber and watercress sandwiches, adding thin slices of bright red radishes and even thinner slices of Parmesan cheese. "Wow, that looks nice," she said with appreciation.

"Well, you and I both know that I'm not usually much of a Martha Stewart, but every once in a while, I get inspired," I said with a grin.

"What is this?" she asked when she opened the lid of the big stainless-steel pot and began stirring the fragrant contents with a heavy ladle.

"It's carrot soup," I answered. "The recipe sounded so delicious that I had to try it. It even has rosewater in it," I said, holding up the bottle.

She smiled as I filled two bowls and carried them to the table.

Hungrily, she sucked the thick soup off the spoon.

"How is it?" I asked as I placed a sandwich next to her bowl.

Tilting her head to the side, she squinted her eyes and shook her head with a puzzled expression. Dipping her spoon in a second time and taking another tentative taste, she hesitated once more. Then, shaking her head with the same puzzled expression as before, she said, "It tastes . . . healthy."

"Oh, boy, that doesn't sound good," I said.

Dipping my own spoon into the soup, I sucked in a mouthful

of the vibrant orange broth. Grimacing, I looked at her and said, "Good Lord! That tastes *disgusting!*"

Without another thought, I grabbed the two bowls off the table and dumped the contents back into the pot. As I rinsed the bowls out in the sink, I suddenly burst out laughing.

"I'm so sorry. I should have tasted it."

With a giggle, she said, "Well, it wasn't *completely* gross."

As time went by, we continued to share what turned out to be much more successful Wednesday-night dinners. We also spent many evenings at each other's homes, chatting. Sometimes we cried as we shared our stories and frustrations, but just as often, we found ourselves laughing out loud at the silliest of things.

One winter, Carlene and I were invited away on vacation with friends. We decided to fly together, and since our flight was scheduled to leave at just before six a.m., Carlene stayed at my apartment, which was only minutes from the airport.

"I didn't sleep at all," she grumbled good-naturedly when I padded out of my bedroom just after four a.m.

My cat, Trix, was gazing at her and purring loudly as Carlene accused, "That two-hundred-pound cat of yours kept walking on me all night. He was even licking my face."

"That's because he loves you," I said, yawning.

With a smirk she added, "And I won't even mention your snoring."

"I don't snore." I laughed as I hurried toward a hot shower.

Within thirty minutes, the two of us were ready to leave for the airport.

When I came out of my bedroom dressed in a pair of blue jeans topped with a white blouse, red camisole, and royal blue fleece, she looked at her own outfit and said, "I look like I'm getting ready to clean out the garage."

"Those jeans *are* pretty beat," I agreed, noting the hole in the knee and the ripped hem. "Do you have anything else?"

When she shook her head, I hurried back into my bedroom and returned moments later holding out a pair of my jeans. I answered the question in her eyes when I said, "They're long on me."

Only fifteen minutes later, we were at the airport checking our bags when the ticket attendant gave me the bad news. "It'll be seventy-five dollars to check your bag."

"What?" I asked, feeling my chest constrict. "Why would it cost seventy-five dollars to check my bag?"

Looking bored, she responded, "Your bag is eleven pounds over the limit."

"That's *impossible*," I said.

The attendant pointed to the scale and raised one eyebrow.

As a feeling of panic set in, I turned to Carlene.

"I'll just throw some stuff out. I don't even need half of it anyway."

When I tossed my suitcase open, she grabbed two handfuls of shorts, T-shirts, and jeans and jammed them into her carry-on. "What are you doing?" I asked.

"I've got room," she answered.

Crisis averted, we hurried to our appointed gate where Carlene settled in with a book. I love people-watching in airports, so I sipped a cup of hot tea and slowly scanned the crowd of waiting passengers.

After a few minutes, I tapped Carlene's leg and said, "That guy over there is checking you out."

"What guy?" she asked, looking up from her book.

"That one," I answered, lifting an eyebrow in the direction of a tall, good-looking blond man with bright blue eyes who was leaning against a pillar, his arms crossed comfortably in front of him.

"He's not checking me out," she said. "He's looking at you."

"No, Carlene. He's not. He's only got eyes for you," I countered.

Just then, our flight was called, and I reached down to collect my carry-on and my purse.

"I'm in Zone One," I said. "So that means I will see *you* on the plane—sucker!"

I fully expected that Carlene would follow me, but when I turned around she was still sitting right where I had left her. Several minutes later, though, she was filing onto the plane, followed by the tall blond, who had engaged her in conversation.

After struggling to hoist her heavy carry-on bag filled with my clothes into the overhead bin, she sat down and fumbled for her seat belt.

"So much for looking graceful," she said, chuckling as she pushed the hair off her flushed cheeks.

"I doubt he cared about that," I said. "I think he was too busy noticing how *fabulous* my jeans look on you."

She laughed, and we continued chatting about the chance meeting until the planed rolled away from the jetway.

As we began taxiing, though, I experienced a sudden sinking feeling, and nausea settled into the back of my throat. I closed my eyes for a moment to consider the richness my friendship with Carlene had added to my life. We had been through so much together, and although I knew we'd always be friends, I had a strong sense that from here on things would be different. Struggling against tears, I turned to her and said, "Carlene, I think my life just changed."

She looked up from her open book and, with a quizzical expression, asked, "What do you mean?"

Both of us hoped to have happy, healthy relationships in the future, and we had talked many times about how we might feel when one or the other of us met someone. Suddenly I was sure that it was *she* who had just met someone.

"That guy you were talking to," I said, gesturing to where he had settled several rows behind us. "You're going to marry him."

The years that followed proved my prediction correct.

Carlene had indeed married John, the guy from the airport, and she would be moving into his house in a few days. It all seemed so surreal—especially since I met the man I would later marry the day before she and John had their first formal date.

Smiling, I met her eyes. "We really have come a long way together, haven't we?"

"And who would have ever thought the two of us would be working on this?" she asked, indicating the piles of stories on the coffee table.

"Pretty cool, huh?" I said as I reopened my laptop, refreshed the homepage, and tapped my scattered notes into a neat pile.

Suddenly, I felt a chuckle rise. "Oh, hey, I forgot to tell you what I brought for dinner tonight."

Her eyes lit up with anticipation. "Is it something good?" she asked.

I couldn't help but laugh when I said, "Well, just for old times' sake, I made us a big pot of carrot soup."

Discovery

Since childhood, I have always believed that women were critical of me. As a result, I was guarded and somewhat defensive around them. Although there were women with whom I was friendly throughout my life, even considering a few of them to be friends, I was careful never to let anyone know too much about me.

When Carlene and I first became friendly, I remained on my guard until enough time had passed and I could see firsthand how she conducted herself in friendship. We shared the same loyalty, sense of humor, and feeling of being honored by the confidences bestowed upon us by other people. Her thoughtful questions often helped me examine emotional situations in my life from a different perspective, and there came a moment when I knew beyond a shadow of a doubt that she was my true friend.

The relationship the two of us have built is the cornerstone of this book. Because I trust Carlene implicitly, I was able to be open to her often-probing questions. Since we came to know each other so well, she was able to sense when I wasn't being completely honest with myself. I am so blessed to have such a beautiful friendship in my life.

Healing throughout this process, I have been able to open myself up to true friendships with women. I am so grateful for the bonds I continue to develop with these friends today.

The heartfelt counsel of a friend is as sweet as perfume and incense.

—Proverbs 27:9 (NLT)

On My Knees

"Please, God, I can't take anymore," I pleaded as a piercing pain ripped through my abdomen. I tried to stand up from the couch but was immediately hit by another, even more intense pain that knocked me right to my knees. As it slowly receded to a dull ache, I was suddenly overcome with a surge of anger. "This is *ridiculous!*" I ranted into the empty living room.

During the previous year and a half, my life had developed into a modern-day version of the biblical character Job. Only months after Gabriel announced his intention to divorce me, a huge tumor had developed in my lower abdomen. "This tumor is every single word I have swallowed over the last year, Gabriel," I said in accusation, pointing to a lump that by then protruded several inches.

Days later, with an incision running from hip bone to hip bone, I winced as I glanced at the photos the surgeon proudly shared. "It weighed over five pounds and took two of us to remove it," he boasted, a broad smile lighting up his handsome face.

Several months after the surgery, I developed double vision and began losing my balance. I wondered if it was the result of being "kicked" into menopause by the surgery, but further tests confirmed that five lesions had developed on my brain, and the doctors were suspecting multiple sclerosis.

Shortly after that, I noticed that all my fingernails and toenails were shredding, reminding me of the potholders we had made as children.

Then one sunny afternoon, as my brother cut my hair he lifted a lock and asked, "What's going on here?" With horror, I stared at a bald spot the size of a quarter just over my left ear. A visit to the dermatologist brought a diagnosis of alopecia, an autoimmune disease that causes balding.

During the past few months, whenever I looked in the mirror, I felt like a human version of a connect-the-dots game, as red marks began to cover my extremities. To make matters worse, my joints were swollen and achy, making it difficult to sleep. It had also become almost impossible to recall even the simplest conversations.

As I was referred from doctor to doctor, several had inquired if there was a possibility that something in my environment was poisoning me. This all ran through my mind as I pulled myself up from the floor. Shuffling back to the leather sofa that now felt cool to the touch, I lay down, praying that I would fall asleep.

Only twenty minutes had passed when I awoke, covered with sweat, my pajamas soaked through. As I forced myself into an upright position, another stabbing pain caused me to list to the right. The glass of water I had tried to sip earlier spilled across the hardwood floor, and my tears began to flow. "I can't do this anymore," I cried quietly as I hobbled to the bathroom, where I folded a washcloth into a cold compress.

Standing in front of the mirror, my face red and swollen, I whispered, "I'm such a mess." By now I was certain I did not have the stomach bug that was making the rounds through my vocal students. This was definitely something more serious. After pulling my saturated pajama top over my head, I removed my shorts, dropping them on the floor. It was when I wrapped the thick bath towel around my body that I noticed swelling in my lower right abdomen. With sudden certainty, I knew: appendicitis.

Although the nearest hospital was only twenty minutes away, I was in no shape to drive there. With Gabriel out of town, I was relieved when I noticed my son Ben's shoes at the top of the stairs. I had been asleep when he'd arrived home early from a camping trip with his friends.

"Ben, I need your help," I whispered into the darkness of his room.

He sat up in bed, rubbed his eyes, and when he saw my face, grabbed the jeans that had been lying on the floor. Gathering me into his arms, he guided me to the door and down the stairs. "I've got you, Mom," he reassured me as he drove me to the hospital.

As I lay on a gurney in the emergency department, Ben and I waited for the arrival of an ambulance that would transfer me to a nearby hospital where I would have surgery. When I worried that my dog, Hannah, and my cat, Trix, would need food and water, Ben said, "Maybe we should call Gabriel, Mom."

With Carlene out of town, no one else but Gabriel had a key to the house, but he was staying with a friend for the weekend. Besides, I didn't want him to know about my predicament.

When Gabriel had announced his intention to end our relationship three years earlier, he had opted to live in the basement of the house we jointly owned instead of moving out. It had been a difficult decision to let him stay, but money was tight. Ben was still in college, and only months earlier I had lost my job due to a merger. When I hadn't gotten another job right away, I decided to start a business. Although the business was doing okay, it wasn't doing great, and I was barely making ends meet.

To complicate matters, only a year before our "separation," he and I had purchased a house that needed significant renovations, and Gabriel was the sole renovator. The house, which was set on a four-acre parcel, needed constant mowing and trimming during the summer, plowing in the winter, and the usual endless maintenance. As my health had deteriorated and I grew weaker, he had cared for me with so much kindness and compassion that I continued to hold out hope he would change his mind and we would resume our marriage. Although I knew the situation was unhealthy, I felt powerless to change it. And now, once more, I was in a situation where I felt there was no other option available. Feeling completely disheartened, I said, "I guess we'll have to call him, Ben. Hannah will need to go out."

As the ambulance rushed me toward the hospital, I gratefully succumbed to a haze of morphine and fell into the welcome release of a dreamless sleep.

When I awoke, Gabriel was standing at my side, a worried expression on his face as he spoke in hushed tones with the nurse on duty.

"She's been sick on and off for a while," I heard him say, his voice warm with genuine concern.

As he was leaving for the restroom a little while later, he gave my shoulder a comforting squeeze and then brushed away an errant curl from my face.

"Don't worry," he reassured me. "I'll be right back."

When he hurried off, the nurse leaned over the bed and, with envy in her tone, whispered, "You are *so* lucky. That man *really* loves you."

I shivered. *Things are not always as they appear.*

Several days later, when Carlene returned from vacation, she hurried up the cellar stairs and into my sunny kitchen. I was sitting on the couch in the adjoining living room, slumped against the pain of the healing incisions. She stopped, regarding me for a quick second before leaning over to examine the healing wound with practiced care.

"Are you okay?" she asked.

"So, so," I responded.

"Well, if it makes you feel any better, I have to tell you, you're looking pretty sexy sitting there all vulnerable," she said, laying her jacket on the couch.

The laugh that escaped tore at my stitches, and I winced. "Funny," I whispered.

She sat down on the love seat, curled her long legs underneath her body, and studied me with kind eyes as Trix settled in against her. Then, dropping her voice, she asked, "Really, Chrissie, how are you feeling?"

"Honestly, Carlene? I'm completely and totally exhausted."

"Gabriel called me today," she confided, glancing toward the backyard where he was working.

"He did? Why?"

"He's worried about you. He told me he thinks you're really depressed, and he's afraid you might hurt yourself."

I didn't have enough energy to be horrified, but I couldn't imagine him believing I would really consider doing such a thing. Shaking my head, I said, "I'm exhausted, but I'm certainly not suicidal, Carlene."

The two of us sat in silence for several minutes, the only sound the hum of the weed whacker as Gabriel trimmed around the garden behind the house.

"Carlene, I can't go on like this," I said as a tear traced its way down my cheek. "Something has to change. Gabriel has been clear about the fact that he doesn't love me, and I hate that everyone sees him as my devoted husband. It's all such a farce. Plus, I'm starting to realize that all these physical symptoms are not going to get any better if he stays here."

She nodded her head in agreement and asked, "Are you still planning to go to counseling?"

"Yes. As a matter of fact, I have an appointment on Saturday morning."

Only minutes later, Gabriel came in from the backyard carrying three ripe, red tomatoes and a cucumber. "Fresh out of the garden!"

he said as he laid the vegetables on the counter. "I'll make salad," he offered, reaching into the kitchen drawer for a knife. Turning his attention to Carlene, he said, "I bought some feta cheese. She loves her salad with feta cheese." Carlene and I shared a knowing look. The entire situation was so wrong.

A few days later, as the counselor listened, I shared the story of my relationship with Gabriel.

"It all sounds pretty toxic," she said, cutting to the heart of the issue with the precision of a skilled surgeon. The counselor was absolutely right. I was embarrassed that she'd so quickly put her finger on the pulse of the problem, so my defenses rose and a wave of heat flushed my face.

"You're upset," she said, her face placid and her voice calm.

"No, I'm not," I answered.

She folded her hands in her lap and searched my face.

"You could start by being honest with yourself, Chrissie."

My back was stiff with tension, and my palms were sweating. I wanted to run out the door and never come back. There was so much I wanted to say in my defense, but instead I held her gaze and said, "It all sounds so simple when you say it."

"It *is* simple," she answered. "What *isn't* simple is how you got to where you are."

No, I thought. *That's all very complicated.*

The counselor and I sat in silence for a few minutes as I considered my options. It was clear Gabriel needed to move out; there was no question about that. But I was haunted by the feeling that, with him gone, I would be completely alone. It wasn't that I would mind living alone, but without Gabriel there caring about me, I would feel as though I had no one. My boys were grown and deserved not to have to worry about their mother, so I kept my problems to myself. Plus, my extended family was not close, and the few times I needed help, no one had been available. Although I knew Carlene would be there for me, she was in the middle of her own heartbreak, and I didn't want to put any pressure on her.

The counselor's expression was serious when she said, "Chrissie, you know this is all up to you, and I think you also know you've got two choices. You can choose to get healthy, or you can choose to stay where you are."

We studied each other in silence for another full minute. I wanted to cry, but I had no tears left. I should never have allowed Gabriel to continue living in the house, but I had been afraid of feeling completely and totally alone. That fear had left me in such a caustic place that I was no longer the vibrant, healthy woman I had been just three years earlier. It was time to let him go.

That night, I experienced an entire range of emotions as I flipped through a box of photos. Gabriel and I smiling and joyful on our wedding day. Benjamin's graduation from high school. Christofer climbing into the U-Haul truck with a wave as he left for school. Our last vacation as a family, playing miniature golf and feasting on lobster. Installing cabinets in the kitchen of our new house. In each photo, we looked so happy.

The next morning, I was nervous when I heard Gabriel's footfalls on the stairs. He smiled when he saw me standing in a pair of jeans, my feet bare, makeup applied, and hair pulled back into a clip.

"You look like you're feeling better," he said as he filled his cup with coffee.

"I am," I answered. There was so much to say, so much that I was feeling. As I pulled in a breath, I sent out a silent prayer. *God, I'm asking that you help me find the right words.* Then, for the first time in a very long time, I looked directly into Gabriel's bright blue eyes.

"Can we talk?" I asked.

"Sure," he agreed, his mood upbeat. "What's up?"

I moved to the table, sat down, and then patted the chair next to me.

"Uh-oh," he said. "This looks serious."

I bit my bottom lip as Hannah cuddled against my leg, offering support.

"It is," I admitted. I didn't waste any time and got right to the point. "Gabriel, I think it's time you moved out."

For a moment, the look of surprise on his face tore at my heart. Through everything that had happened, I still loved this man.

"Why?" he asked. "I love it here."

I took a few seconds to remind myself that it was he who had stepped away from the marriage. Plus, he wasn't saying he loved *me*. He was saying that he loved *our property*. Steeling myself with a deep breath, I continued, "Look, you know I've been really depressed, and having you here just makes it worse. I think it's best that you go."

He stood up and began pacing the kitchen floor, his face etched with doubt.

"But you've been so sick. Who's going to take care of you?"

"Me," I asserted. "And, if need be, Carlene is only a few miles away."

His uncertainty fortified my confidence.

"I appreciate your concern, Gabriel, but I think that while you're here, I'm not going to get better. I also want to finalize the divorce," I added.

It was then that his anger flared. "You can't handle this place by yourself, and I don't want to sell it," he insisted.

"Then you can move back upstairs, and I'll move out," I answered.

He puffed out his chest and pulled himself to his full height. "I think this is a really *bad* idea," he said.

We held each other's gaze for several very long seconds. When I said nothing, he made up his mind.

"Fine. I'll do whatever you want. When would you like me out?"

"How long do you think it will take you to find a place to live?" I asked.

He shook his head. "I don't know."

"I would like a deadline, Gabriel. Maybe you could stay with your mom for a few weeks."

Once more he met my eyes full on. *Don't blink*, I willed myself as I stared back at him. This had to end. Today.

Finally, he said, "Fine," and leaving a barely touched cup of coffee on the counter, he turned on his heel and bolted down the stairs.

Only moments later, I heard the engine of his truck burst to life. With a mixture of sadness and blossoming hope, I watched him pull out of the driveway and disappear around the bend.

Although I knew I had a difficult road ahead of me, and I was still dealing with doubt and fear, I was on my knees once again that night. The difference was that this time, I was saying a prayer filled with gratitude and relief.

Discovery

This experience proved to me that our mental and emotional health have a direct effect on our physical body. Within the first eight months following Gabriel's announcement of his intention to file for divorce, I developed a large tumor in my abdomen; from there, over the next three years my health continued its steady decline. Because I was riddled with fear and anxiety over the challenges I was suddenly forced to face on my own, I allowed myself to feel trapped in a toxic situation in which I felt powerless. It wasn't until I reached my mental, emotional, spiritual, and physical breaking point that I was finally able to confront my fears and ask Gabriel to move out of the house we shared. Only a few weeks after he'd moved out, my physical body began to respond positively, and I started the long path back to overall good health.

What I also discovered through this process is that Gabriel's acts of kindness when I was physically ill were reminiscent of my dad caring for me when I was sick as a child. In both cases, I took the love where I could get it and ignored the damaging behavior that had made my body sick in the first place.

I have come to understand that our bodies cannot rationalize or make excuses for unhealthy situations in our lives. It is our responsibility to be attentive and responsive to signals of distress, especially when the stress lasts over an extended period. Respecting ourselves and our bodies requires that we make changes—sometimes difficult ones—before the body reaches a painful breaking point. However, when change doesn't come as quickly as we hope, I have learned that being brought to our knees puts us in a position of strength, for it is from there that our greatest transformation often occurs.

O LORD my God, I cried to you, and you have healed me.

—Psalm 30:2 (AKJV)

At the Falls

The house that Gabriel and I had purchased together six years earlier was sold. I had spent the previous month finding a place to live and sorting through my belongings. I would be moving into a much smaller place, so I was donating books and clothing to local groups who were still recovering from Hurricane Irene. The house had been scrubbed from top to bottom, and Gabriel had installed a new ceiling fan in the bedroom for the buyers, who were thrilled with their purchase. I was excited about moving to the duplex I had found. It seemed perfect for me—small enough that I wouldn't feel like I was rattling around in a big, empty space, but big enough that I wouldn't feel claustrophobic. The landlord had been a little hesitant when I told him I had both a dog and a cat.

"A cat is fine," he said. "But I'm not so sure about a dog."

It may have been the disappointment on my face that caused him to reconsider. "Does she bark?" he asked.

"Only when the doorbell rings," I assured him. "She's a really good dog."

The backyard was perfect, too. Several big trees hung over the property line, and a huge oak tree shaded the front lawn. Carlene and I had cleaned the windows and hung curtains, and I was ready to move on to a new life—a new beginning.

The day before I was to move, I woke up and jumped out of bed with a plan. During a leisurely breakfast, I scribbled in my journal, signing and dating the entry. When I finished, I opened one of the boxes that was stacked in the kitchen near the door and began rummaging through it.

"Here it is," I said to Hannah, who was eyeing me closely. From the box, I pulled a candle, two small stones, a glass candleholder, and a bundle of sage and then laid them on the kitchen table. "I wonder what I did with my backpack . . ." I mumbled into the quiet kitchen. "Oh, I know."

Running down the cellar stairs, I grabbed the pack and then hurried back into the kitchen, where I carefully placed everything into it. Not quite satisfied, though, I dug deep into the corner of the still-open box one more time.

"It has to be here," I muttered, smiling when my fingers wrapped around a small, reddish-brown crystalline stone.

Less than ten minutes later, gravel crunched under the wheels of my car as I drove into the parking lot. Stepping out, I looked around. It seemed impossible that I hadn't been here in nearly six years. The passing years had marked the lot with muddy potholes and weeds that had sprouted through the heavy clay underlay. The railroad ties that used to be piled with careful precision had spilled over, and vines had grown over them. As I looked around, a chill ran over me.

When I opened the back door of my car, Hannah bolted out. By the time I had reached into the backseat for my pack and closed the door, she had hurried down the overgrown path toward the falls.

"Hey! Wait for me!" I called as I ran to catch up.

When I found her, she was standing at the swollen stream tentatively dipping her paw into the water. I don't know if it was anxiety or excitement that washed over me when it struck me that the stream was a metaphor for life: liquid, always moving, even though at times it appeared frozen solid or dried up—continually clearing a path and leaving things behind that were no longer needed.

I stopped for a moment as I thought about the big pile of packed boxes in the cellar containing items that had been earmarked for donation. Those "things" had seemed so important at one time, but their significance had been lost as my life had changed.

I shook my head as a moment of nostalgia washed over me. I hadn't been alone here in almost thirty years. In the past, I had always come with my kids, a friend, an occasional family member, and, once, a lover. I smiled at the memory and then glanced toward a trembling Hannah.

"You're fine, girl," I reassured her.

She glanced at me and then once more contemplated the rapidly flowing water before hurrying forward. She slipped, falling into the chilly stream before finding her footing on a wet, mossy rock. Eyeing the space between her and the shore, she carefully picked her way across with me close on her heels.

"You made it!" I cheered as she shook her damp fur. With one glance backward, she took off at a dead run toward the falls.

The air around me was crisp and cool, and the leaves on the trees overhead were tinged with yellow. That fall, I was feeling the change of seasons more deeply than I had in a very long time. It seemed nearly impossible that a short six years earlier, I had been so happy and content in my life.

Memories sprinted through my head as I followed Hannah up the steep trail toward the falls. Yanking on the waistband of my jeans, I thought, *I should have grabbed a belt.* I had battled with my weight my entire life, but in the last year the pounds had just fallen away. "When you let go of the weight of the past, the pounds will follow," a healer friend had suggested when I told her what was going on with my body. Ten pounds had gone in one year.

When an exposed stone caused me to trip, I grabbed a small tree to prevent myself from falling. "Damn it," I cursed when the thick bark of the tree cut my palm.

"You shouldn't use foul language," Carlene had joked one afternoon as we sat chatting in her apartment. As I walked, I explored the word *foul: F-o-u-l,* "paltry language." *F-o-w-l,* "poultry language." I couldn't help but giggle. *It feels so good to be happy!* I thought.

On the heels of that memory came another—one that had been playing on a loop in my head: A crisp breeze had whistled around the side of the house as I'd watched my son Ben pulling away, waving. I had tugged my heavy flannel work shirt closer to my body to ward off the chill. As Ben's car disappeared around the bend, my then-husband Gabriel had come up behind me and wrapped his arms around my waist. Together we stood looking out over the valley beyond. As he nuzzled my neck, he had whispered the words that would haunt me for years: "We're going to share this view for the rest of our lives, Chrissie." I had leaned into him, loving his scent and the way his cheek felt against mine. We had swayed in that spot, reveling in the warmth of each other's bodies for several minutes. I had never felt so happy, so secure, or so loved. I wanted to stay right there in that moment, forever.

Instead, we moved apart, kissed, and went back to our separate chores. It was only months later he made the announcement that would send us on to our separate lives.

I heard Hannah whining further up the trail, so I picked up my pace. "I'm coming, girl!"

She hurried on ahead to where I could hear the water crashing over the falls into the pool below. As I scaled the hill and stood at the edge of the path, I noticed that the pool seemed smaller and the shore bigger and rockier than I remembered. It occurred to me that it had been a dry summer, soon forgotten after two full weeks of rain.

Far below, Hannah was prancing along the shoreline chasing something that I could not see from where I stood. I hurried down the path to stand at the edge of the rocky shore, the echoes of many summers gone by resounding in my head.

"Mom! Look! I skipped the stone *three* times!"

We had spent so many summer afternoons there—me with a

book, my kids running through the pool trying to catch small fish or locating the dry stones in the narrows that would serve as a bridge to the ledge on the other side. I had always carried a magnifying glass so that, if the opportunity presented itself, we could inspect the red spots on the back of a green grasshopper or the thick hairs on the leg of a big black spider.

I squatted down to stare at my reflection in the still water of the shallow side of the pool. Years earlier when I had knelt in that same spot, I noticed the first lines etched into my face. *Smile lines*, I thought. But still, that night I had stopped at the cosmetic counter on the way home to buy my first jar of anti-wrinkle cream. I remember thinking, *I have no issue with growing older, but I'd like to do it gracefully!* I reached down and drew the word *happy* on the surface of the water, and it rippled out to the other side before disappearing under the falls.

It had been there at the edge of the pool that my boys and I had shared blueberry muffins and cooled tea while we talked about the fact that their dad and I would be separating.

My son Christofer's face had been sullen, his eyes dark and angry.

"You gave up your right to be happy when you had kids, Mom," he had said, his voice low, his teeth clenched. He had believed that. I hadn't disagreed. It was that exact thought that had held me for years in a place where I was unhappy because I had feared that he might be right.

I was quickly brought back to the current moment when a redtailed hawk swooped down from an old pine tree near the lean-to, swiftly ending the life of a chipmunk that had let its guard down for a moment too long. Life and death, right there in front of me. *Everything really can change in a heartbeat*, I thought as the bird disappeared beyond the tree line.

For a moment I closed my eyes, and when I opened them I was once more transported to a time many years earlier. It had been a cold February afternoon when my son Ben, his friend Andrew, and I had braved the icy path to the falls. The transformation there had caused us to pull in our breaths in surprise before letting out whoops of joy. The falls were frozen solid, and the sun overhead broke into sparkles and shimmers of light when it hit the thick icicles.

"It looks like a lion's cage!" Ben had shouted over his shoulder as he hurried forward. Both boys had gotten right into the game, roaring and growling with all the gusto of nine-year-olds.

"Come on, Mom! You be a lion, too!" Ben had begged.

"Not me!" I had called from across the frozen pool. "No cages for me!"

Andrew's happy answer had melted my heart when he said, "Then you be a bird! Birds can fly out of cages!"

The wind ruffled my hair, bringing me back to the moment. Pulling my hands from the warmth of my pockets, I placed the backpack at my feet and unzipped it. Hannah hurried over, sniffing at the contents of the bag and sneezing when I held out the small bundle of sage. Digging deep into the pack, I removed the candle, holder, and matches. The match blazed on the first strike, but it fizzled in the brisk breeze. The second strike did no better. *Patience*, I thought, closing my eyes for a moment to center myself. My reason for being at the falls that day was an important one, and I wouldn't let the wind or anything else get in the way of my plan.

On the third attempt, the match lit, and I shielded the flame with my hand, quickly bending to touch the wick of the candle. As the candle spit and sizzled, I dug into the pack for the carefully chosen stones. I had found one on a lonely walk along a beach in Rhode Island the previous fall and another while I hiked a steep incline on Mount Shasta earlier that year. The last stone I found on a piece of property I hoped to purchase in Kinderhook, New York. With the candle lit and the stones laid out around it, I picked up the small bundle of sage and lit it from the flame of the candle. The sweet-smelling smoke rose upward, tickling my nose.

"Smells good, doesn't it, Hannah?" I asked as she lay down on a grassy spot nearby.

Holding the smoldering sage in my hand, I swiped it first over my feet and then around my body and over my head. It was my purpose that day to hold a ceremony as a way to say good-bye. But it was not my intention to say good-bye to the memories I held so close to my heart. Instead, I was symbolically releasing the parts of me I no longer needed—the parts that had held me captive in a cage I had created with my own thoughts and words. It was time to let go of the past—time to honor the person I had become. With my small altar complete, I once more looked around the pool and over to the falls. I was ready. Drawing my journal from the pack, I opened it to the page I had dog-eared earlier that morning and laid it at my feet. Then I raised my hands upward and closed my eyes.

"My Dearest Creator, I am here today to thank you for bringing me to this place. I do most truly appreciate the love, the pain, the hardships, and the teachers who have guided me to this point. I am here in your presence in this beautiful place that has brought so much joy to my life, and I ask you to witness this act of casting away all that I no longer need. I am thankful for the lessons I have learned and for the great gifts I have received in return. Today I am proclaiming my love for the one person who is your greatest gift to me in my life. That person is *me*. I have written a letter as a vow, and God, I ask that you witness this promise I make to myself."

Dropping my hands, I once more picked up the journal and scanned the words I had written that morning. Suddenly a wave of emotion ran over me—one that was the strangest blend of excitement, sadness, and nostalgia. As a crow called out over my head, I took a long breath, and in a confident voice I began to read.

Discovery

My visit to the falls was to mark the end of a period of deep intro-spection with a ceremony of celebration. By then I had begun examining the detrimental patterns that had been holding me back from becoming the person I believed I was capable of being. This ceremony was a way to honor the Divine Spirit that had been with me throughout this time, supporting me and fueling my desire and motivation to persevere even when I felt like giving up. The ceremony was a rite of passage during which, with *intention*, I began to let go of thought patterns, relationships, and emotions that no longer served me.

> *Now faith is the assurance of things hoped for,*
> *the conviction of things not seen.*
>
> —HEBREWS 11:1 (ESV)

Thirty-Three First Dates

James was tall. James was handsome. James was charming.

"You're so beautiful," he said when he took my hand, turned it over, and planted a light kiss on my palm. My heart fluttered. It felt so good to be admired after so long. He and I had met at a business function two weeks earlier, and he had followed up with a phone call several days later. "I'd like to take you to dinner," he'd said. I had been flattered, and now I was excited for a fun date.

"A bottle of your best champagne," he said, smiling at the waiter before adding, "and a plate of oysters."

The table was decorated with a light blue tablecloth and soft yellow flowers that seemed to lend an air of sophistication to the experience. When the champagne arrived minutes later, the waiter made a show of uncorking the bottle and then pouring a small amount for James to taste.

"Delicious!" he affirmed.

The waiter filled my glass, and I settled in to enjoy a beautiful evening.

Sipping champagne, we chatted easily. James was interesting, accomplished in business, and well-loved in the community. He was a family man whose children were now grown, with children of their own. We had spoken a number of times on the phone since we met, and I was finding myself smitten.

"Chrissie," he said, "I really like you."

Once again, my heart fluttered, and my cheeks blushed pink. He was wonderful, and his long, lean body and rugged good looks were an added bonus.

"Thank you, James. I like you, too."

Just then, the oysters arrived. As the waiter turned away, James spoke again. His blue eyes sparkled as he said, "I've given this a lot of thought, and I've decided that I like you enough to be completely honest with you." He sipped his champagne and, after dropping an oyster on his plate, reached across the table to once again take my hand. "The truth is, Chrissie, I'm married."

I pulled my hand away, sitting up straight in my chair, too stunned to speak.

"But she and I have an arrangement," he continued, his eyes hopeful.

Without skipping a beat, I reached into my purse, handed him my phone with a smile, and said, "Let's call her to verify that."

The date was over before even one oyster had passed my lips.

"He's married, Carlene!" I said, still unable to fully understand how someone could be okay with dating another woman while he was married.

"He's married?" she asked.

"Yes."

"I can't believe it," she said.

"Me, either. Can you imagine me sitting there getting *that* bombshell dropped on me? I almost threw up. He said he has an arrangement with his wife, so I pulled out my cell phone and offered to call her," I said with a giggle.

When the laughter died away, Carlene became serious.

"Wow, what a disappointment."

James was date number one. By then, I had been separated from Gabriel for nearly five years, and although I wasn't fully into the idea of dating in my fifties, I was just beginning to feel the twinges of loneliness. I hadn't given much thought to what I was looking for in a mate, but I absolutely wasn't interested in dating a *married* man.

That first very discouraging experience led me to the decision to employ a dating service, one that specialized in matching professional people. The organization was reputable, promising that each candidate was screened before being matched with other clients. Once I'd signed my name to the contract, the dating began in earnest.

The next date that stands out in my mind was Mike. Mike was date number five. We were to meet on what turned out to be a beautiful August afternoon, so I chose my favorite summer sundress and a pair of strappy sandals to match.

When I arrived, the hostess was excited.

"This is my first time making an introduction for the dating service," she confided. "Follow me. He's in a booth in the back. And he's gorgeous!" Her excitement was contagious.

He sat engrossed in a video on his phone, not noticing for several seconds that we stood there waiting to get his attention. When he looked up, the hostess said, "Mike, this is Christina. Christina, this is Mike."

She was right: The guy *was* gorgeous. He was tall and muscular, and his dark hair framed stunning blue eyes. As he shook my hand, though, it was clear from his expression that the admiration was not mutual. He slid back into the booth and made an announcement. "I want to be clear that I'm not interested in supporting anyone at this point in my life."

Suddenly my pretty blue sundress and cute heels seemed the wrong choice. Did I look like I couldn't afford a new dress? He spent the next hour and a half regaling me with stories of his ex-lover, a highly paid lawyer. "She made bank," he repeated at least a half-dozen times.

When the evening was over, though, he surprised me with a warm hug. "You seem like a really nice person, Christina. Good luck with this whole dating thing."

"I definitely don't want to be with a man who's going to view a partner as a burden," I said with a laugh when I called Carlene after the date.

"He sounds like a real winner," she said in a comforting tone.

Somewhere between date number five and date number nineteen, I met a sixty-year-old anesthesiologist still pining away for his former girlfriend, a twenty-eight-year-old who had taken him for a house and a racehorse before moving to Florida to be near her ex-lover.

Then there was Jerry, one of the sweetest men I had ever met.

For me, there was no chemistry, though, so after getting together a few times, I politely refused any further invitations.

One Saturday morning, I shared coffee with a poet, who—although I never saw him again—continued sending me his writings for another two years, even though I never responded.

Then there was Charles. Charles was a guitarist who was thrilled when he found out that I, too, played guitar and sang. His excitement was infectious.

"I'll call you tomorrow," he offered. "We'll get breakfast. Bring your guitar, and we'll find a place to play."

I never heard from him again.

"Maybe he had a heart attack or something," I said the next day when Carlene called.

"Or maybe he was hit by a car, and all of his fingers got broken," she responded.

"Broken fingers?" I laughed. "That's no excuse!"

Date number nineteen became the man I dubbed "The Meatball" due to the huge plate of spaghetti he consumed during dinner and his lack of social graces. I arrived at the appointed time at an upscale Italian restaurant not far from my home. The hostess, a grim woman with a permanent sneer, escorted me to the table where he sat, buttering a piece of bread.

"You're late," he said, not getting up.

"I was told to be here at seven o'clock," I said, checking the time on my cell phone.

He sniffed, turning his eyes to the menu while I sized him up. He wore a dark blue, pinstriped suit. The collar of his shirt was open, and his neck was decorated with numerous gold chains. *Oh, boy*, I thought, when he complained to the waiter that the butter was too hard.

As he chewed on a thick crust of bread, he said, "I have to be careful. Women are after me for my money."

"I wouldn't even know you had money unless you told me," I said. "And besides, to me, a man is measured by his ethics and moral values, not the size of his bank account."

He rolled his eyes and then turned his attention back to his plate. "I make *well* over six figures." From there he launched into a monologue describing his numerous income streams, ending with a dissertation on the exorbitant child support he paid his ex-wife.

She deserves it, I thought. I was having difficulty spending two hours with this man. I couldn't imagine having spent nearly eighteen years with him.

As he droned on, he painted a picture of what he was looking for in a future mate. I paid close attention, studying him as he spoke. When I couldn't keep my mouth shut any longer, I shared my thoughts. "I'm wondering why you're dating."

He looked up, his expression confused. "What do you mean?"

"Well, from what you're telling me, it seems you could just hire yourself a cook and a maid and save yourself the possibility of another round of child support."

He sat up straight in his chair, his dark eyes glowering. He was angry when he shot back, "If I had known dating would be like *this*, I would have never left my wife."

"Maybe she'll take you back," I countered with an innocent smile. He must have found my wit interesting because when we parted ways in the parking lot, he asked to see me again.

"Oh, my God, Carlene! He had at least twenty gold chains around his neck! Totally not my type. Besides, I'm not interested in being a highly paid maid and housekeeper."

But as I snickered, I suddenly started feeling guilty. Why was I being so mean? He was just some guy trying to figure out what he wanted. So he wasn't a match for me; he was probably a match for someone.

The next memorable date was with Jeff, who earned the title *The Fastest Date in History*. When I left my house to drive to the appointed spot, I dialed Carlene's number.

"What date number is this?" I asked.

It was she who had started keeping track more than a year earlier. Numbers were easier to remember than names. "Let's see," she said. "I think this is date number twenty-nine."

"Okay. Wish me luck."

When the hostess introduced us, Jeff stood up to shake my hand with a dour expression.

"I'm sorry if I'm not into this tonight," he said as he sat back down, picking up a beer that was already on the table. "I'm having surgery tomorrow."

"Surgery? Why didn't you cancel tonight? We could have rescheduled."

His smile was strained. "No, a couple of beers will help calm me down."

Conversation was like pulling teeth—or I should say it was more like pulling toenails.

"What kind of surgery are you having, if you don't mind sharing?" I asked.

"I have an ingrown toenail," he all but whimpered.

With a smile, I joked, "Sounds serious."

"You never know," he said, a pained expression on his face. "I could lose my foot."

With that, he swallowed the last of his beer, excused himself, and limped toward the door without looking back. The date was over in less than fifteen minutes.

As I drove home, I thought about the information the dating service had given me about him. "You'll love him," she'd promised. "He's a very accomplished man. He's a published author who has traveled all over the world." But over his beer, he shared that he wrote for a local rag, and he dreamed of someday traveling to Florida.

Carlene's voice was incredulous when I called her.

"The date's over? That's got to be a record."

"Date number twenty-nine lasted barely fifteen minutes," I replied.

"So, you were supposed to meet him for drinks, and it turned out to be a shot?" she joked.

"A shot! Funny." I laughed. Then, turning serious, I said, "That guy completely misrepresented himself to the dating service. I definitely don't want a dishonest man."

Several months later, I met Jackson, date number thirty-three. It had been a horrible day, and I would have postponed except for the fact that I'd already put our date off once. As I entered the restaurant where we were meeting, I checked my outfit in the mirror behind the bar. It was perfect: slim white slacks, a feminine blouse, and a pair of heels Carlene and I had picked out together. But I hated my hair. A trip to the hairdresser on my way to the date had turned out to be a really big mistake.

"Easy on the product," I had warned as my hairdresser slathered his hands with humectant and mousse and then rubbed them through my hair.

"Stop being so difficult." He laughed, his eyes shining. "In this weather, it will make your fabulous curls even more fabulous."

He was right about the curls: They were perfect. But my hair felt sticky and heavy. *I* felt sticky and heavy. The humidity clung to my skin, making my mood as dark as the skies outside the window where I sat sipping a cup of tea with lemon while I waited for my date.

"He just called," the hostess announced when she bounced to my table. "He's running ten minutes late." Then she added, "He sounds nice."

"Thank you," I said, forcing a smile before returning to my thoughts. I was busy contemplating all the reasons I wished I had canceled tonight. First, there was my hair. Second, my mood. Third, there was a stack of work on my desk that was piled halfway up the window. Fourth, there was the fact that I was getting sick to death of meeting men and continually being disappointed. *Maybe I should come to terms with the fact that I'll probably spend the rest of my life alone,* I thought. But the truth was that my heart was crying out for a loving companion.

Only minutes later, the hostess bounced toward me again, this time followed by an attractive man dressed in a striped blue button-down shirt and a pair of khakis. His dark blue eyes smiled, and I immediately liked his open way. He looked like fun. My mood brightened in an instant. He shook my hand, pulled out his chair, and sat down across the table, smiling at the hostess. "I'll have a cup of coffee," he said, after glancing at the white mug in front of me.

"The woman at the dating service told me you're her favorite," he said, his voice enthusiastic.

"Really? Well, that was very sweet of her."

"And she said you would be a real catch."

Now I chuckled. "I've been paying her off for a while now. It sounds like she's finally doing her job."

His laugh was hearty. We chatted easily for close to half an hour, sharing our individual stories of how we ended up meeting for a blind date on a cool, rainy evening.

When the waitress returned to check on us, he ordered a glass of wine.

"Would you like menus?" the waitress asked.

I glanced at him. "Yes," he said with confidence.

I smiled, nodding my head in agreement. "And I'd like a glass of wine as well. Chardonnay, please."

As she walked away from the table he asked, "How do you think this is going so far?"

I think it was the intensity in his eyes that caused me to take a breath. "So far so good," I answered.

"I think so, too," he said.

Conversation flowed, but I became concerned when I couldn't seem to get a question in edgewise.

"How many children do you have?" he asked.

"Two," I answered. "They're both grown now."

"Boys? Girls?"

"Boys."

"Do you get along with them?"

"Very well."

"What do you do for work?"

"I work with an advertising agency."

"Do you like it?"

"Most of the time."

"What does that mean?"

"It means I'm like anyone else. Sometimes I love my job, and sometimes I'd like to stay home with my head under the pillow and forget about it."

"Your head under the pillow? What do you mean by that?"

"I mean that there are days when work is overwhelming, or the clients are giving me a headache."

"You don't like your clients?"

"Of *course* I do. But some days they're ridiculous in their demands."

"Ridiculous? What do you mean by that?"

And the questions continued until it began to feel like an interrogation. After about fifteen minutes, I was completely frustrated, and I had the distinct impression that his questioning was a way of protecting himself from talking about his own life. When I had had enough, I said, "I don't want to answer that."

"Why not?"

"Because I think it's an inappropriate question for a first date."

"Why would you say that?"

"Because that's a subject I would only discuss with a friend."

"But how will we get to know each other if you don't answer my questions?"

Suddenly I was feeling defensive. I had answered every one of his questions, but so far, all I knew about him was that he could come up with questions faster than I could come up with answers. So, I deflected his question with a question of my own.

"How many kids do *you* have?"

His expression changed quickly, and his eyes closed to slits. Suddenly I felt like we were locked in competition—one we were both intent on winning.

He fired a volley. "Why are you avoiding my question?"

My jaw clenched. I deflected his volley. "Why are you avoiding mine?"

Our determined eyes held for several very long seconds. By then I was sitting up straight and stiff, while he bent forward, his right palm on the table.

He who speaks next, loses, I thought.

Suddenly he flashed a brilliant smile, and the tension dispersed.

"Three. I have three children," he answered.

Now I was trembling. What had started off as fun had gone bad quickly, and it was becoming clear that I didn't like this guy. I was getting the sense that he was arrogant, and arrogance was a characteristic I despised.

As dinner continued, he ordered another glass of wine.

"Would you like another?"

"No, thank you," I answered.

"Bring the lady another glass," he said, winking at the waitress.

I shook my head in her direction. "No, I'm going to need to drive home."

"Not for a while," he countered, checking the time on the cell phone next to him. "It's only seven-thirty."

The waitress searched my face as I shook my head in frustration. Finally, I agreed.

His smile was victorious.

At around eight o'clock, he opened up about his business, laughing as he told a story about one of his more-humorous clients. Then he shared an account of a recent meeting from which he was carrying some residual displeasure. "You seem pretty savvy," he said. "What do you think about the outcome? Was I right?"

Without hesitation, I offered an opinion that was fueled by my annoyance. "I think that's what happens when you need to be the smartest man in the room, Jackson."

To this very day I can recall that moment like I am still in the middle of it. In an instant the expression on his face went from confident, swaggering businessman to that of a wounded little boy. *Apologize!* my heart reproached. *You had no right.*

But as quickly as the wounded look had run across his face, anger replaced it. It was then that my brain took over. *No apology necessary. He deserved it.*

Moments later, he motioned to the waitress. "We'd like some cheesecake." Then he tossed me a challenging grin, adding, "And bring two spoons."

The next day, I had a bad-date hangover.

"He was awful," I sputtered to Carlene on our morning call.

"How so?" she asked.

"He was so arrogant. I can't stand men like that."

I couldn't admit—even to her—that he had left me intrigued.

Discovery

Although dating could be discouraging, effortful, and often frustrating, I learned that it was an important step in the process of self-discovery. Through each date, I was conscientious about remaining self-observant, noticing that sometimes I spoke my mind without thinking and that I talked too much and didn't ask enough questions. I also noticed that I had a tendency to focus on business and career rather than the personal aspects of my dates' lives. On a positive note, though, I was told by many of my dates that I had a nice way about me that put them at ease.

I also learned that I jumped into dating like it was my job—a job with an end goal of meeting an emotionally healthy, compatible partner. By treating it as a job, though, I focused on the objective rather than on the adventure of meeting new people. That mind-set dampened my ability to fully appreciate and enjoy that unique time in my life.

Not long after I began dating, it became clear to me that I was great at identifying what I did *not* want in a partner. It took me many months to realize that it was necessary to take the time to identify the qualities and characteristics that I *did* want in a mate. By considering the positive aspects about dating, it became an easier and better experience overall.

The best part of dating was having a trusted friend there to support me, just by being there to confide in. When I grew discouraged, Carlene was there for comfort, and I could count on her for honest feedback. She also provided another perspective, one that was invaluable to me. Although occasionally there were tears of disappointment, Carlene and I were usually able to find some humor in my dating situations. To this very day, we continue to look back at those experiences and laugh.

Guard your heart above all else, for it determines the course of your life.

—PROVERBS 4:23 (NLT)

Again? Really?

I couldn't get Jackson, date number thirty-three, out of my head. When he handed me his card at the end of our first date, I wanted to rip it up and throw it at him. Instead, I tapped it on my steering wheel the entire ride home and then laid it on my nightstand, picking it up to look at it as soon as I got out of bed the next morning. He had left me feeling off-balance, but he had also left me intrigued. I was finding it impossible to wrap my mind around my muddled feelings.

Inwardly, I cringed when I recalled the words I had so casually thrown at him. *I think that's what happens when you need to be the smartest man in the room.* But the thing that really bothered me was that, even though the expression on his face told me I had wounded him, I hadn't been able to bring myself to apologize. All through dinner, I had been so self-righteous, judging his arrogance, but now I was worried that maybe I was the arrogant one.

"So, I take it you won't be seeing him again," Carlene said when we chatted the next morning.

I couldn't imagine seeing him again, but the feeling of uncertainty made my heart race. There was a part of me that wanted to know more about this guy, and I was too embarrassed to admit it.

Jackson's business card sat propped up on my desk at the office. Because I didn't really see us going on another date, I had spoken with my coworkers about him as a possible business opportunity. So far, though, I hadn't followed through.

"I wish you'd call him," one of my coworkers pressed. "You said yourself he doesn't have an ad agency, and I've looked at his marketing materials. We could add some real value."

I, too, had looked at his website, but for a different reason. I had found myself studying his photograph on the front page. Somehow, he seemed familiar, although I was sure our paths had never crossed. I would have remembered him.

Feeling conflicted, I once more brought his company website up on my screen. My coworker was right. We could add some real value to his marketing efforts. And besides, I was a professional, one who had never let her personal feelings get in the way of reaching out for new business. So why was I hesitating?

Under my coworker's questioning gaze, I said, "Okay, you're right. I'll shoot him an e-mail right now."

I began typing: "Dear Jackson. It was nice meeting you a few weeks ago, even though it was obvious that you and I are not a match. Would you mind if my business associate reaches out to you? We've looked at your website, and we've got some ideas we believe will increase your site traffic."

Only minutes later, I received a response: *It was nice meeting you, too. And I want you to know that I don't agree that we're not a match.*

It felt as though my heart stopped. I reread the line several more times. *I don't agree that we're not a match.* It took a few moments to shake off the small thrill that ran through me before I could continue reading. *Yes, please have someone contact me.*

Only weeks later, his company signed a contract, and our team began creative brainstorming sessions. We spent hours preparing the pitch presentation, but on the day of the face-to-face meeting at his office, I had second thoughts.

"I don't want any involvement in this account. I'll help where I can, but you guys can handle it."

My coworkers were confused. "Are you sure? You worked so hard on this."

I nodded. "I'm positive," I answered.

The arrangement was perfect until a few months later, when my coworker called.

"Jackson wants you at the meeting tomorrow."

I shook my head. "Well, I'm not going. You can handle it."

"He's being insistent."

The next day, I walked into Jackson's office and shook his hand, meeting his eyes with all the confidence of a capable businesswoman. But my hands were cold and trembling as I followed him from his office to the conference room. To make matters worse, this man, the one listening intently to the input of his staff and showing off pictures of his grandson, was a very different man from the one I had met across the dinner table months earlier. If I was ever going to be comfortable around him, I would need to apologize.

On the way home from the meeting, I made a quick decision to call him, figuring I would leave him a message. He picked up on the second ring. My mouth went dry, but quickly a river of words rushed out.

"Jackson, I'm calling because I am embarrassed for the part I played in a really awful first date. I realized today that I will never be comfortable around you unless I let you know that I'm sorry for what I said. I had no right to judge you."

His voice was kind when he responded. "That's very nice of you, Chrissie."

I was immediately relieved. Then he said, "I'll let you off the hook if you tell me why you did it."

Without thinking, I said, "Well, since I'm being honest, I'll tell you that I thought you were the most arrogant, self-centered man I had ever met."

His laugh was immediate and hearty, sending another wave of relief through my body.

"Is that it?" he asked.

"Pretty much," I said with a giggle.

I could hear the warmth of a smile in his voice when he said, "You're honest, Chrissie. I like that."

We chatted easily for nearly half an hour before he asked, "What are you doing tonight?"

My mind froze and then went into flurry of swirling thoughts.

If he was intending to ask me out on a date, there was no way I could go. He was now a client, and dating a client would be completely unprofessional. "Let me see."

My heart was pounding as I feigned checking my calendar. I needed to buy a little time while I reasoned out what to do. Finally, I answered, "Oh, I'm sorry, I have a meeting tonight."

His response was quick. "How about tomorrow?"

"Hmm . . ." My calendar was completely devoid of any social engagements for the next month, and I already knew that.

"Are you there?" he asked when I didn't answer right away.

"Oh, sorry—dead zone," I answered. The part of me that was intrigued by him won out, so I finally answered, "Tomorrow would work."

"Great. I'd like to take you out to dinner," he said.

My stomach lurched. He *was* asking me out on a date, and I found that I did want a second chance to make a good impression, especially after witnessing the open, caring man that he had been in the office that day.

"Are you sure that's a good idea?" I said. "I've been told I'm a barracuda."

He gave another hearty laugh. "Why not? We'll pretend the first date never happened. It'll be a do-over."

When I arrived at the agreed-upon restaurant the next evening, it was just after six o'clock. He stood in the parking lot, waiting under the bright halogen light. As I stepped out of my car, he hurried to help me, closing the door behind me and then escorting me forward with his hand against the small of my back. Once inside, the conversation flowed, and dessert came too soon.

As we walked back to my car, I thanked him for the do-over.

"It was fun," he agreed, smiling as he pulled me toward him. My heart thumped hard in my chest as I studied his square jaw and intense eyes. Suddenly, he lifted my chin and planted a tender kiss on my lips—a kiss I knew I would never forget. His breath smelled of coffee, his face of cologne, and his leather jacket was soft against my cheek when I laid my head on his shoulder. I wanted to stay there forever.

As winter wrapped us in a cold blanket of snow and ice, we spent several evenings a week together. It had been a very long time since I felt attractive to a man.

"You're beautiful both inside and out," he complimented me as we shared meals and talked late into the night. It wasn't long before I was completely at ease with him. He was interesting and fun—but I had also noticed that he could be very moody.

One evening late in February, while we sat watching a movie on his couch, he was distant, his brow furrowed. I wasn't surprised when he reached for the remote to shut off the television and then turned to meet my gaze. There in the dark blue of his eyes was a deep melancholy very similar to what I had seen in another set of eyes, one that had ultimately led to heartbreak.

"I have to tell you something," he said, his voice sounding tired.

When he hesitated, I spoke for him. "You're in love with someone else."

His eyes opened wide in surprise and then cast downward. Nodding, he said, "I'm really sorry, Chrissie." It was then he shared the story of a breakup that was more than a year old but whose wound was still fresh.

My mind was suddenly on full alert. *Leave! Now!* But the hurt in his eyes was so genuine, so honest, that I sat rooted right there. We remained in silence for several minutes before I admitted, "I'd be lying if I said I wasn't disappointed." The chemistry between us was easy and electric, but with another woman in the picture, there was no basis for us to build a relationship.

Finally, I stood up from the couch, dragging on my heavy parka. "I should go."

His voice was apologetic when he asked, "Would it be selfish of me to ask you to stay?"

"Yes," I answered gently. "It would."

I grabbed my purse and my keys, but he looked so miserable that I hesitated. *Just go*, my head cautioned again.

I started toward the door where I stood with my back to him for a full minute before turning back around.

"If you really love her, Jackson, you need to find out if she's still interested in you. Maybe she would be open to coming back."

"She's not," he answered. "I've tried."

I moved across the room, kneeling in front of him. "I'm so sorry. I know how it feels to love someone and then lose them."

He hugged me hard, practically squeezing the breath out of me. When he loosened his grip, I stood up, walked to the door, and, after one long glance backward, closed it behind me.

It was several weeks later that I entered his office for a regular monthly meeting. Since the night of his confession, we had not communicated. I missed our conversations, especially his joyful laugh.

"How have you been?" he asked, shaking my hand.

I hated to admit that I had been looking forward to seeing him. His eyes were the same dark blue I imagined every night as I fell asleep. With a smile, I answered, "I've been good."

The meeting was over too quickly, and the drive home seemed long. Later that night, a text pinged my phone. "Can I call you?"

I sat for several minutes, staring at the message, torn between excitement and distress. *This is why you don't mix personal with professional*, I thought. My mind ran over all the reasons not to let him call, starting with *He's in love with someone else.* But I wanted to talk to him, and I reasoned that he might want to discuss an agreement I had left him to sign on my way out the door, so I answered, "Sure."

When the phone rang moments later, his voice purred over the line. "I've missed you."

But you miss her more, I thought.

I felt as though I were choking on my conflicted emotions. Jackson was everything I didn't need in my life, but on the other hand, we had such an easy way between us. *Be careful*, my mind warned. *You've been down this road before—twice.* The seconds seemed like hours as I struggled against my feelings. Finally, I spoke.

"I've missed you, too, Jackson."

"Have you missed me enough to have dinner with me tomorrow?" he asked.

My pulse immediately began pounding like a bass drum in my head. This was the last thing I needed, but it was the only thing I wanted.

"Jackson, I would love to have dinner with you, but I am not interested in playing second to another woman."

I didn't expect what he said next. "I went to see her."

"You did?" I didn't want to know what happened.

"Yes," he answered. "I went to see her a few days after you were here last." He paused, and quiet hung between us. After several long seconds, he explained. "She's living with her old boyfriend, and she seems happy."

"How do you feel about that?" I asked.

"I'm happy that she's happy."

"But are you *over* her?" I pressed.

When he burst out laughing, I was reminded of why I liked him so much.

"You're so serious! It's just dinner!"

When the man was in a good mood, he had such joy—a joy that spilled over like a fountain, bubbling out to everyone around him. And maybe he was right. Maybe I *was* too serious. Maybe I should just go and have a little fun. I only hesitated for a second before agreeing.

As I drove home, I considered calling Carlene but decided against it. I knew she'd be worried if I told her I was going to see him. But later that night, she called me, and as usual I couldn't help but be honest.

"Are you sure you should go, Chrissie?" she asked, her tone uneasy. "You know he didn't answer your question, right?" I thought about how happy I was to have the opportunity to see him again. But she pressed, adding, "He didn't say he was over her; he only said he was happy she was happy."

Suddenly I giggled, my mood light in anticipation of my date.

"You're so serious, Carlene. It's only dinner!"

Not long afterward, the warmth of spring brought with it the returning birds and colorful tulips. On one such day, Jackson took me flying in his small plane. Together we soared over the trees in a cloudless sky.

"You looked so happy up there," he said after we landed. He pulled me into a warm embrace, kissing my brow and murmuring, "I'm so glad I was able to do that for you." I leaned on his shoulder, and murmured, "I love you, Jackson."

Weeks went by, and although he and I talked every single day, I hadn't seen him since the day we had gone flying. One afternoon as we chatted, I asked, "Jackson, when am I going to see you again?"

He laughed. "If you want to see me, all you have to do is ask, Chrissie."

"Okay, how about tomorrow?" I suggested, in challenge.

"That would be nice," he agreed. "It's going to be a beautiful day, so I'll take you flying again."

We hung up with a promise that he would call in the morning to discuss the details.

That evening, I went to Carlene's for dinner.

"Chrissie, are you in love with him?"

"I believe I am, Carlene."

She was quiet, and I could feel her caring disapproval. We had had several discussions about the fact that Jackson rarely asked me out on a date but instead invited me to his house, which was just over an hour from mine. By then, even those invitations had stopped.

"He should be courting you," she insisted.

On the one hand, I knew she was right, but on the other, I was accepting the relationship on his terms. I had decided that, for now, it worked.

"Oh, come on, Carlene. He's not that bad," I said.

But she remained serious, and silence hung between us for several seconds.

Her voice was gentle when she said, "Are you sure he's not just your usual type?"

The following morning, I woke up early, excited to see him. But he never called. All day I was distracted, continually checking my phone for a text or voicemail. As the sun began to dim and evening rolled in, I finally grew angry. It wasn't up to me to ask him out or track him down. He had promised we'd go flying, and then he didn't even have the decency to let me know why he hadn't followed through on his promise.

That night, I crawled into bed at eight o'clock and cried myself to sleep.

Close to midnight, a text pinged my phone, sending a luminescent white glow onto the nightstand. Through puffy eyes, I read the message that was only two words. "My dad."

I picked up the phone and, without a moment's hesitation, called him.

"I'm so sad," he said, his voice breaking as he shared the news of his father's death.

In less than ten minutes, I was in my car, making the hour-long drive.

Several days later, I was in his kitchen, preparing us a hot meal. I chose my words carefully. "I would have liked to have been at the funeral to support you, Jackson."

He relaxed against the kitchen counter and forced a boyish grin. "You could have come."

"You didn't invite me, and you know very well that I didn't have any of the details."

"You could have looked in the paper. It was in the obituaries."

"I wouldn't have come without an invitation, Jackson. You know me better than that."

He studied me as I met his eyes and then pushed himself away from the counter to wrap me in a hug. "What matters is that you're here now, right?"

My face grew warm as suppressed anger rose in a teary wave. *What am I doing here?* I thought. In that moment, I felt like I meant nothing to him. But several days earlier, I had felt like I was everything to him as he lay in my arms, crying out his grief over the loss of his dad. The situation was too complicated, and I was exhausted. To make matters worse, I couldn't help but wonder if he hadn't invited me to the funeral because he hoped his ex-girlfriend would be there.

I didn't meet his eyes when I said, "Jackson, this relationship isn't working for me."

His reaction was immediate. "Please, don't do this to me, Chrissie. I can't lose you right now."

When I met his eyes, his face crumpled, and within seconds his body was wracked by heaving sobs. As he sank to the floor under the weight of his grief, I dropped right along with him. Holding him in my arms, we both cried for completely different reasons.

The following week, he called. "Come for dinner, and bring your guitar? I'd really love to hear you sing."

That evening as I drove toward his house, a message pinged my phone.

Text me when you're close. I'm having a glass of wine at Andy's.

When I was about five miles from his house, I pulled over and texted back. *I'll be there in a few minutes.*

Moments later, he responded with a smiley face.

But when I arrived, he wasn't there. After thirty minutes, I texted again. He replied, *On my way!*

A half-hour later I called, this time leaving a message on his voicemail. "Just checking that you're okay, Jackson. I'm getting worried."

Another forty-five minutes had passed before I finally decided to leave. As I backed out of his driveway, his car pulled up next to mine and he tossed me a friendly wave.

I fired him an angry glance and then looked away.

"Where are you going?" he called.

I shook my head as I headed toward the main road.

He turned his car around and came after me, flashing his lights. I stopped just before turning onto the highway.

"I'm sorry," he said, bending into my window, smelling of wine and cigars. "I got tied up."

"At Andy's?" I glared at him. "Jackson, I've been waiting for you for almost two hours. I'm hungry, I'm crabby, and I need to go home."

There was a genuine apology in his voice when he said, "Please. I was really looking forward to dinner."

I hated that I loved this man. Over and over, his behavior displayed his self-absorption, but asking me to dinner and then leaving me waiting in his driveway was downright disrespectful. I shook my head, not meeting his eyes.

"Look, this was wrong of me," he said. "But I'm having such a rough time, Chrissie. I need you. Please. Don't go."

I stared at my steering wheel trying to decide what to do. I wanted to leave.

"Chrissie. *Please*."

I knew I should go home, but the tug on my heart caused me to turn my car around and follow him into the driveway where I had just spent the last two hours alone.

A week or so later, he called early one afternoon, his tone all business.

"I'm considering switching advertising agencies. There's an

agency in New York City that has pitched me some really great ideas."

While he wasn't courting me, I thought, *a competing agency has obviously been courting him.*

"I'd love to share the ideas I got from them and get your feedback."

Really? I thought. *You want feedback on the work of a competitor?*

"What purpose would that serve, Jackson?" The edge in my voice was unmistakable.

His answer was quick, a challenging retort. "Maybe it would save you my account."

Several tense seconds passed before he spoke again, this time in a conciliatory tone.

"Look, Chrissie, the New York agency is not a done deal. Please come over. I'll make us a nice dinner."

When I didn't respond, he pressed.

"You always have such a great perspective, and I would really appreciate it."

Hours later, he met me at his door with a warm hug and a glass of cold wine.

"It's so good to see you," he murmured into my ear.

Dinner was delicious, and it was clear he had gone to great pains to make a nice meal, but I struggled to enjoy it. As he finished clearing the table, his smile was warm.

"Let's sit down and take a look at the mock-ups," he said.

With some pageantry, he laid the artwork across the dark coffee table. I examined the colorful graphics, studying each piece with an industry-educated eye as he assessed my reaction. Finally, I said,

"These are okay, Jackson, but none of it is anything special."

He grinned. "I agree," he said, adding, "They're ordinary." Then he reached back into the big envelope and pulled out one last graphic. "But this one is good," he said, holding it up.

When I read the slogan that was splashed across the top of the page, my body stiffened.

"Jackson, this is the exact same campaign we pitched to you when we started working together last year. I happen to know that for a fact, because I am the person who came up with the idea."

His intense eyes bore into mine, daring me to look away, but his challenge only fueled my indignation. Flicking the artwork with my finger, I said, "You didn't like it, Jackson. You said it was too soft."

He smirked, looking back at the colorful artwork in his hand. "Well, I like it now." Then he nodded his head, this time with a Cheshire grin. "As a matter of fact, the more I look at it, the more I like it."

Standing up from the couch, I pulled in a long breath, and then announced, "Jackson, I think it's time for me to go."

For a second, he looked confused. "Why?" he asked.

Was it possible that he really didn't understand what he was doing? *No way*, I decided. *He's a very smart man. He knows exactly what he's doing.*

As I collected my sweater, I said, "Jackson, when I met you on our first date last year, I was looking for a partner."

With his eyebrows knitted into an angry line, he spat back, "You never said that."

Just as quickly, I asked, "Isn't it implied when two people are dating?"

The tension between us seemed to last forever. But slowly, I softened. I was the one responsible for letting this unhealthy relationship go on for as long as it had. I had never ended a relationship with an angry exchange, and I wasn't about to start now.

"Maybe this is my fault, Jackson. I honestly didn't know what I wanted when we first met. But it was so nice to love someone after feeling nothing for so long."

I paused, looking around the room, knowing that I would never return.

"I'm a very loving person, Jackson, and you know that. I want to be with someone who really cares about me." My eyes moved to the artwork he still held in his hand and then over to the coffee table, where many colorful printouts lay scattered. I could hear the sadness in my voice when I murmured, "It's clear that you *don't* care about me."

He jumped to his own defense. "I *do* care about you."

"Not in the ways I need," I countered.

As I picked up my purse, I turned to meet his eyes for the last time and said, "Jackson, I'm leaving."

His gaze followed me as I dug for my keys. "Chrissie, please, you don't need to go."

"Yes, Jackson, I do."

As I stepped out the door for the last time, the bright light of the full moon lit the way to my car. I turned the key in the ignition, put the car in drive, and pulled away.

And this time, I didn't look back.

Discovery

Although it appears that this story is about my relationship with Jackson, in truth it is about my relationship with myself. Of all the stories in this book, this one has been the most difficult to admit. By the time I started dating Jackson, I was sure that I would no longer be attracted to a man like him because I believed I finally understood my own worth. But even though I knew better, I once more fell into my old pattern and allowed him to treat me disrespectfully.

It wasn't until I dissected my relationship with my father through this discovery process that I fully understood why I was attracted to this type of man. What I've realized is that growing up with my dad's changeable moods and volatility made me comfortable around an unpredictable personality because I knew how to deal with it. I even prided myself on my ability to defuse an explosive situation by bringing a highly charged emotional moment back to a place of calm. I now recognize that, for me to neutralize these situations, I was usually making excuses for bad behavior, discounting my own feelings, and allowing compassion to overrule my understanding of a healthy relationship. I fell in love with Jackson because I made a choice to focus on the redeeming parts of his personality while ignoring what I recognized as unhealthy.

Now let's get down to the fact that once more I stayed in a relationship where I knew very early on that he had residual feelings for another woman. I now understand that I continued to date him because as a child, I believed that I needed to *prove* that I was worthy of love. As a result, in my mind I rationalized that even if the man I loved continued to have feelings for another woman, as long as I was the one he was calling and to whom he was showing his affection, the situation was tolerable. In each case, I believed that, in time, I could *prove* to him that I would be the better choice.

I also now understand that what I perceived as bad behavior from Jackson was just that. I have since learned that many people who have suffered trauma have difficulty with discernment because they do not have healthy personal boundaries as a reference point. When children's needs and boundaries are respected, they are able to develop a "sixth sense" that helps them understand when a relationship is not quite right. This is a skill that will carry through into adulthood.

There are many of us who would like to believe that becoming whole and healthy is as simple as taking the three or five or ten easy steps that are outlined in some self-help books. In reality, though, these steps are rarely consecutive, and they are not easy. Even so, there is a happy ending to this story. Through the course of deep introspection and lots of prayer, I was finally able to understand that until I truly recognized and embraced my own self-worth, no one else would, either.

For though the righteous fall seven times, they rise again …

—Proverbs 24:16 (NIV)

Making a List

Intelligent, nice, gentlemanly, affectionate but not smothering, witty, emotionally available, respectful, trustworthy . . .

Carlene and I had worked on the list for hours, making it as specific as possible, even adding deal-breakers, which were the characteristics in a possible partner that I wouldn't accept. Several weeks after the list was complete, the dating service called with a new candidate.

When I entered the restaurant on the night of the date, a young maître d' smiled and gestured to a rack where I could hang my heavy winter coat. As I followed him into the dining room, he led me to a booth where a handsome gray-haired man sat sipping a glass of wine. The maître d' nodded, making the introductions. "Chrissie, this is Rick. Rick, this is Chrissie." Rick smiled, scooting out of the booth to shake my hand.

I sized him up quickly. There was something kind about the

softness around his eyes, and although I detected an air of confidence, the slight trembling of his hand when he released mine exposed some nervousness. The dating service had told me he worked as a chief systems engineer for a corporation in Pittsfied and that he was a musician, so I knew just the subject to set him at ease.

"I understand you play guitar," I said. Within minutes we were both relaxed, and I settled in to enjoy the easy flow of our conversation.

Likes music, I thought. *Check.*

As dinner was served I said, "So, Rick, I was told you're a widower."

"Yes," he said. "My wife and I were happily married for more than thirty years." He explained that she had died from cancer. His eyes were soft when he shared that his adult children had moved into the house to support him and their mother during the last ten days of her life. "The kids were great," he said. "Even my future son-in-law was there."

Strong family connection, I thought. *Check.*

As the evening wound to a close, he sipped a cup of coffee after dessert, smiling when I asked, "So how has your dating been going?"

Leaning slightly forward, he said, "You tell me. You're my first date since 1978."

I wasn't even out of the parking lot before I called Carlene.

"How did it go?" she asked.

"It was really good. He was very nice, but there's one *minor* detail to consider," I joked.

"What's that?" she asked.

"He said I was his first date since 1978!"

"You're kidding me!" she said with a giggle.

"Figures, huh?"

The two of us burst out laughing. Then, recalling the effortless flow of our conversation, I added, "He was nice, though. I liked him."

"That's good," she said, her tone supportive. "Nice is on your list."

True, I thought. *Nice. Check.*

As much as I would have liked to see him again, though, it only made sense to me that a man who had been married for more than three decades would want to date a lot of women before settling on one.

"Who knows if I'll ever see him again," I said.

"I wouldn't rule him out just yet," Carlene's tone was encouraging. "Did you give him your card?"

"When I pulled out my wallet to give him my card, there weren't any more. But he did give me his," I said.

"Are you going to reach out to him?" she asked.

I wasn't sure, but after having a week to think about how easy it had been to be with him, I decided to e-mail him.

His response came quickly. "It's nice to hear from you. I enjoyed meeting you, too, and would love to see you again."

After several e-mail conversations, he sent some ideas for a next date. As I perused the list, I was impressed. He had obviously been listening during our dinner date because the list included all things I liked to do. We settled on a concert followed by dinner.

Good listener and wants to court me, I thought. *Check.*

Dinner after the concert was fun, and the two of us shared lots of laughter throughout the meal. Later, as we wandered to the parking lot, Rick admitted that by the end of our first date he thought I wasn't interested in him. "I thought you were letting me down easy when you didn't give me your card."

"I really didn't have any!" I laughed. "Besides," I continued, "I assumed you'd want to meet at least a hundred and fifty women before deciding to go on a second date with anyone."

He threw his head back in a hearty laugh. "No, I'm not that kind of a guy," he said, his eyes twinkling.

Easy laugh, I thought. *Check.*

The following week, he called to ask if we could spend a day together.

We met for a quick lunch before heading into the mountains, where he owned a camp on a serene lake. "Go ahead and relax," he said, pointing to a chair at the water's edge as he pulled another one over for himself. For several minutes, we sat hunched against the early spring chill, listening to crows off in the distance.

"I was brought up Catholic, too," I offered when he shared that he and his wife had gone to parochial school together.

"I was an altar boy," he said.

A spontaneous burst of laughter escaped me, and I blushed at his look of surprise.

"I'm not laughing at you," I explained. "It's just that my sister and I used to love to wink at the altar boys. We had so much fun making them nervous." I smiled at the memory and then continued.

"I don't go to church as often as I used to, though." As my eyes took in the beauty of the mountains beyond the mirror-like surface of the water, I smiled. "These days I find God in places like this."

Suddenly his smile faded, and his expression turned serious.

"I hear you," he said, adding, "I haven't been to church since my wife's funeral. Giving her eulogy was the hardest thing I ever did." We sat in silence for a few minutes as we studied the horizon. "But I do believe in God. And I've always had a strong connection to Mother Mary," he added.

Inwardly, I smiled.

Spiritual. Check.

When a chill set in, we packed the chairs into the bed of his truck and headed back to his house. As I was leaving, he asked, "Would you like to get together again next week?"

"Sure," I said with a grin. I was feeling good about how our relationship was developing. But it was when he suddenly leaned in to lay a kiss on my lips that it felt as if time had stopped.

This can't be! I thought. Hurrying away, I scrambled into my car.

"He's the worst kisser *ever*," I whispered into the phone as I was backing my car out of his driveway.

"What?" Carlene asked. "Why are you whispering?"

"I don't know. Maybe I just don't want to hear myself say it," I answered.

"Why was it so awful?" she asked.

"I don't know. It just was. I'm so disappointed. We had such a nice time."

"There must be a reason it was so bad," she said. "Did he slobber?"

"No," I answered.

"Did he open his mouth too wide?"

"No, that wasn't it," I said with a snicker.

"Was it his mustache?"

"I don't think so," I answered honestly.

"So, what was it?"

"I don't even know," I said. "It was just bad."

"Maybe he was nervous," she offered. "It's obviously been a long time since he kissed anyone other than his wife, and you know the first kiss can be awkward."

She had a good point. "You might be right. But I was just so shocked. To make it worse, I feel bad because I *bolted* out of there. I'm not sure I even said good-bye."

We burst out laughing.

"So now what?" she asked.

"Honestly, I don't know. He's such a nice guy, but that was bad . . . *really* bad." Shaking my head at the memory of the lackluster kiss, I couldn't help but giggle again. "We're going to get together again next week, so I guess I'll give it one more shot."

The following week I was nervous when he once more leaned in to kiss me.

He's not a good kisser . . . he's a great *kisser!* I thought with happy relief. *Check!*

A few months later, Rick decided to come home early from a two-week vacation to accompany me to a party. But when he arrived at my house that morning, I wasn't feeling well.

"I'm sorry," I apologized. "I don't think it's anything major, and I'm sure I'll be fine before it's time to leave for the party."

As he sipped a cup of coffee on the recliner while relating the high points of his trip, I suddenly realized, with a sense of horror, that I was going to throw up.

"Excuse me," I said, making a display of nonchalance as I headed toward the stairs that led to the downstairs bathroom. Over my shoulder, I tossed the words, "I'll be right back."

As soon as I was out of his sight, I ran as fast as I could, barely making it to the bathroom before I was sick.

Throughout the next couple of hours, I was sick several more times before finally admitting to Rick that I was ill and needed to lie down for a bit. I finally dozed off on the couch, and when I opened my eyes, Rick was still sitting in the recliner, quietly reading a book.

Patient, I thought. *Check.*

When I glanced toward the window, I noticed that the light coming through it was dim. Confused, I squinted at the clock, trying to see through blurry eyes. Four-thirty! By now, the party had been in full swing for nearly three hours.

"This is so embarrassing," I said, fighting the tears that were always just below the surface when I was sick. "You drove all the way back from South Carolina just to go to this party with me, and here I am, sick as a dog."

He moved from the chair to the couch where I lay shivering. Pulling a second blanket over my body, he touched my forehead.

"It's not a big deal. You certainly can't go to a party if you're sick." Glancing at the clock, he said, "You probably should try to eat something."

I shook my head; the thought of eating anything made my stomach roll.

"I'll go get us some food. That way it will be here once you feel well enough to eat."

Later, after a light dinner of rice with soy sauce, I wasn't feeling much better.

"I'll stay," he said, when I decided I needed to go to bed.

"That's not necessary," I said. "I'm a big girl. I'll be fine."

"I really don't mind," he reassured me. "I can't leave you here alone when you're sick like this."

Kind, I thought. *Check.*

The following week, we made plans to have dinner together. When I met him in the parking lot of the agreed-upon restaurant, I could barely muster up a smile.

"I have to be honest, Rick. I almost canceled. I don't think I'm going to be good company tonight. I've had the worst day ever, and I'm in a really bad mood."

Undaunted, Rick smiled, took my hand, and led me through the restaurant door.

"Don't worry about it," he said as the hostess led us to a small table in the back. "Everybody has a bad day now and then. Maybe it would help you to talk about it."

A couple hours later, after a delicious dinner and great conversation, I was smiling and relaxed.

How nice. I thought. *He's a good communicator. Check.*

I was touched when he said, "If this is how you are on a bad day, I'll take it."

"Really?" I asked.

He nodded his head, his eyes kind. "With me, you can be who you are. Partnerships are about two people being honest about their feelings."

Partner person. Check.

Through the summer months, we continued sharing dinners, long walks, time at his camp, and lots of good conversation. One day late in August, after a trip to the mall, we sat in my small house, the late-afternoon sun slanting in through the window. I could hear the air conditioner straining against the humidity, and even though it was set on high, I was still very warm.

"Do you want a soda?" I asked. "It's pretty hot in here."

He shook his head and smiled. "No, thank you," he said. "I'm good."

"Okay," I answered, flopping myself down on the couch and running my fingers over my big cat, Trix. I smiled at Rick across the room where he once again sat in my favorite recliner.

Suddenly his eyes turned thoughtful. Raising his left hand up from where it rested on the chair, he extended it toward me.

"Chrissie, I would like to invite you into a relationship with me."

Surprised, I sucked in a quick breath. No one had ever invited me into a relationship before.

He's such a gentleman, I thought. *Check. Check.*

By now, I knew that, Rick, like me, was not a casual dater. A relationship meant something to him. He was so much fun, and from what I had seen, he was a very good man who was smart, educated, and had made something of himself. Beyond that, he was meeting all the criteria on my list. I was determined to break my pattern of choosing the wrong guy, so I considered his invitation carefully.

"Are you sure you don't want to do a little more dating first?" I asked.

"I'm sure," he answered. "I've dated enough women to know that I got the cream of the crop right out of the gate."

He thinks I'm a real catch. Check.

I moved across the room to perch myself on his lap, contemplating his thoughtful eyes. He was doing everything right.

"Okay, Rick." I grinned. "In that case, let's give it a go and see what happens."

"Thank you," he said. "I'm looking forward to doing just that."

The list looked so good on paper, but despite how much I enjoyed Rick's company and appreciated all his great qualities, I was still struggling to understand why I felt as though there was something missing.

Discovery

Making a list helped me to not only clarify the qualities that I felt were important in a partner, but also to highlight those characteristics I would consider "deal-breakers." To be sure I stayed on track,

I kept the list pinned to a bulletin board over my desk as a daily reminder. I trusted that by making the list and checking it twice, this time I would recognize naughty . . . and finally choose nice.

Getting wisdom is the wisest thing you can do! And whatever else you do, develop good judgment.

—Proverbs 4:7 (NLT)

Checking It Twice

"You can't treat me like I'm not here," I said.

My hands were shaking in anger, and the heat rising in my face was warming the freezing cabin of his truck. "What kind of guy doesn't help the woman he claims to love when she's struggling to climb over a snowbank? And you didn't do it just once," I added. "You did it the other night, too."

We drove in silence for more than fifteen minutes as my mind replayed the events of the last few days. It all started three days earlier when Rick's son, Scott, had called to announce that his wife, Liz, was in labor. "The doctor said the baby will be here around nine o'clock," Rick had said when I walked in the door of the house we shared.

I glanced up at the kitchen clock. Six-fifteen. My head had exploded with thoughts as I struggled to find the right words. I hadn't been able to bring myself to meet his eyes when I said, "I don't know, Rick. I'm not sure it's appropriate for me to be there."

This was the first big family event since Rick's wife, Jean, had died, and I was uncomfortable with the idea of being there. His children, Scott and Susan, had welcomed me into the family, but I knew I was no substitute for their mother, especially at an event as important as this one.

Rick's expression had turned hard for a few seconds before it softened.

"Look," he said, "you're my support person now. I need you there."

While I understood his feelings, I was still uneasy. But I wanted to do the right thing by him, so I answered, "If you're sure."

His face wore a slight frown when he said, "I am."

Flipping his keys into the air and then grabbing them with his gloved hand, he headed toward the door.

"Scott made dinner reservations for the family for six-thirty. The plan is to meet him at the hospital after that."

The conversation around the table had been lighthearted, pulsating with anticipation.

"This is so exciting!" Susan said with a giggle. "I'm going to be an aunt! Tonight!" She glanced at her phone and then announced with a grin, "Better finish your beer, Dad. It looks like the baby's coming now."

Rick chugged down the last sips in his glass and then reached for his coat. He and Susan walked arm in arm, their long legs in perfect sync, while I picked along the icy sidewalk behind them.

Just under an hour after our arrival at the hospital, Jacob made his appearance.

"He has a full head of black hair!" Scott had announced when he threw open his arms to receive a hug from Rick and me. Only moments after Jacob's birth, they all encircled his squirming little body and he was received as a full-fledged member of their family.

When the hands on the clock had pointed to ten, I whispered, "I think we should go, Rick. Liz is exhausted."

Rick picked up his coat from the chair, and as we started toward the parking lot, Susan joined us. Once more, she and Rick walked arm in arm and then hugged each other hard before separating. She whispered into his ear before climbing into her car, and he smiled, his face tender.

Unlocking the driver-side door of the truck, he climbed in and turned the engine over while I shivered in the cold.

I tapped on the window. "Did you forget somebody?"

He glanced at me, unlocked the door, and once I climbed in, put the truck into reverse, waving at Susan as she drove away.

When we pulled into the driveway of our house, it had been treacherous. The snowbanks that were piled high after last week's storm had melted in the day's sun, but as the temperature had dropped below freezing, everything had turned to crunchy, slippery ice. *Geez,* I thought as Rick slammed the door of the truck and headed to the house without so much as a glance toward me. *Thanks a lot.*

By the time I had maneuvered across the driveway and gotten myself inside the house, he was nowhere in sight.

A little while later, when I made my way to the bedroom, I whispered, "Are you awake?" When he didn't respond, I listened for the long pull of breath followed by a rattling exhalation that indicated he was sleeping, but there had been nothing. In the dark, I dug my pajamas out from the dresser and then climbed into bed. "Good night," I whispered.

The next morning, he was already gone when I woke up at five-fifteen. As I drove to work that morning, I thought about what had happened the night before. I knew Rick loved me, and as difficult as the situation was, I had known it wasn't going to be easy when I got involved with a man whose wife had died. So far, he had been very good to me, and my sense was that he was genuinely a good man.

That night after dinner, I had asked, "Do you want to go to the hospital to see the baby tonight?"

"No," he answered, not taking his eyes off the laptop computer screen that was set up in the middle of the table.

"Okay," I replied. I had paused, hoping he might explain. After a short time, I asked, "Did you hear from Scott?"

"Yes."

"How's Liz?"

"She's fine."

He was not making this easy. "And Jacob's fine, too, I'm assuming."

"You would have heard if he wasn't."

Minutes later, he had disappeared into the bedroom without a word. This time, though, I followed him. "Are you okay?" I asked, my voice soft.

"Yes," he said, keeping his eyes fixed on the page of the book in front of him.

Moving closer, I sat down on the edge of the bed. "I can't imagine how hard it must be for you to experience the birth of your grandson without Jean."

Without saying a word, he looked over the top of his glasses and then back to the book he held low in his hands.

Although I was frustrated by his lack of communication, I knew he was struggling with his feelings, so I decided it would be best to let it go. I would bring it up in the morning.

But once again, he was gone when I woke up.

Later that day, I received a text from him.

"They're taking the baby home. We'll stop over at Scott and Liz's tonight."

"Liz is going to be exhausted. Are you sure that's a good idea?"

"Yes," he replied.

"I love you," I typed, adding a bright red heart.

Once again, we had grabbed dinner at a pub in Pittsfield. Rick was quiet as he sipped a beer and ate a thick burger. I wished he'd say something—anything—but despite my attempts at conversation, he remained withdrawn.

When the waiter filled my water glass, I had shivered.

"Could I get water with no ice?" I asked, explaining, "I'm freezing." *And not just due to the weather*, I thought.

Before I had even finished my salad, Rick stood up and pulled on his coat.

"Scott and Liz are waiting. Are you ready?"

My patience was running thin when, once we arrived, he again left me to navigate a snowbank, closing the door of the house behind him while I struggled in the cold.

By the time we left Scott and Liz's an hour later, I was ready to blow. Climbing into the truck and settling on the seat as close to the passenger window as possible, it was a couple minutes before I could find any words. Finally, trembling, I asked, "Rick, do you have any idea how hard it is for me to be the one who is here witnessing the birth of your grandson, when I know full well that not only you, but your entire family, would have rather had your wife here?"

He glanced sideways at me and then fixed his eyes back on the dark road. The muscle in his jaw clenched and unclenched, but still he said nothing.

As we drove in silence, the full moon was hanging high overhead. It lit the interior of the truck with a misty glow, turning everything to a shimmery silver. It could have been magical and romantic. Instead, it was stifling.

Finally, he spoke, his voice low and tinged with anger.

"It doesn't matter what I want," he said. "She's not here. She's *dead*." His grief was palpable, even though his face remained steely.

Suddenly I could no longer contain my anger, so I didn't hesitate before I retorted, "Well, I *am* here and I'm *not* dead."

What a horrible thing to say, I thought.

I steadied myself with a deep breath and then in a kinder voice explained.

"Look, I hope you understand how very difficult this is for me, too. I'm trying to figure out what to say or what to do." Shaking my head, I reached my hand to gently touch his leg. "Rick, I want to do the right thing, but I have no training in any of this."

His words were red hot when he fired back, "I don't, either."

We rode in strained silence, the seconds turning to minutes while his hands clenched the steering wheel, his knuckles white. My body was stiff with tension, and I sat with my back ramrod straight.

His next words hit me hard.

"Chrissie, you need to understand that I have a hole in my heart that you'll never be able to fill."

Suddenly I was infuriated. How dare he think he was the only one who had suffered?

"Nice," I fired back. "And what makes you think that *your* hurt is so much worse than mine? Can you answer me that? Your wife died. Yes, that's sad. But with your loss, your family rallied around, they made you meals, cleaned your house, they applauded your dating. When my husband left, no one rallied around me. No one even cared, and my heart was completely broken."

I gasped in a breath as another wave of hurt and anger roared through me. I couldn't help but add, "At least your wife didn't *want* to leave, Rick. She wanted to stay. But my husband *did* want to leave. To make it worse, he had a whole list of reasons why he felt he was *justified* in leaving. So, what am I supposed to do with that?" My heart pounded, causing an explosion of pain in my head. "I have a hole in *my* heart, too, Rick."

"It's not the same thing at all," he shot back, glaring at me.

"No," I agreed. "It's not. From where I sit, it's worse."

"Sure," he snorted. "Of course that's your opinion."

This time I got out of the truck first, slamming the door with all my might. I stalked over the slippery driveway, not caring if I fell. *Screw him*, I thought.

I flicked on the porch lights and stamped across the dark kitchen to the refrigerator. I threw the door open. Grabbing an apple, I dug my teeth into it with an angry crunch and then spat the chunk out in the garbage.

That night I could not bring myself to lie near Rick on our king-size bed. I clung to the seam on the left side, my hand tucked between the mattress and the box spring to ensure I wouldn't roll near him. I slept only in fitful bursts, my mind running crazy. I loved Rick, but all night his words rang through my head. *There's a hole in my heart that you will never be able to fill.* At least he was being honest.

Losing a spouse, especially one who had been his childhood friend, had been traumatic, but it seemed, up until then, as if he had recovered well. From the very beginning of our relationship, I had had nagging doubts about his emotional availability—doubts that he and I had discussed. He reassured me time and time again that he was in a good place and ready to start a new life. But suddenly I was feeling that my doubts had been confirmed.

Dinner the following night was quiet. We ate in silence, both of us lost in our own thoughts. As I sipped a cup of tea, he cleaned the table and loaded the dishes into the dishwasher. I listened as he ran a cloth over the kitchen counter and then the stove. While he worked, I kept my eyes on the pages of the book in front of me, even though I was not absorbing a single word of it.

I was taken by surprise when he came up behind me to plant a kiss on my head and then pulled a chair in front of me, his knees touching my leg.

"I thought about what you said," he announced.

Raising my eyes to meet his, I immediately forgot about the book in my hands.

"You thought about what?" I asked.

"About whose hurt is worse."

My heart jumped, and I felt my face grow warm. "And?" I asked.

"Well, I realized that you're right." His eyes were thoughtful as he studied my face. "I've always been judgmental about divorce." He hesitated and then touched my hand before continuing. "It was my belief that people who were divorced just didn't try hard enough. I thought they were taking the easy way out."

"And now?" I asked.

"Well, I realized that it's true: Some people do take the easy way out. But many others don't. Many people are victims of their circumstances."

A wave of relief ran over me. *My patience has not been wasted on this man*, I thought.

"I'm sorry about the things I said last night and for the way I've been treating you. Sometimes life deals us some bad blows, and we're left with the aftermath. Jean and I had a great life, and there will be times that I miss her."

"I know," I said. "That's normal, and it's the way it should be."

His eyes remained thoughtful, so I continued.

"Of course I can't fill the place in your heart where you hold your memories of your life with her. There's so much love there, and it taught you so much."

He nodded in agreement.

"I have a hole in my heart, too, Rick," I added. "But it's okay. There's still plenty of room for you."

He nodded, reaching for my hand. "I'm happy with what we're building, Chrissie, and I'm grateful that I'm with you now. It's important to me that you feel you are a part of my family."

My face grew warm as I breathed away a rush of tears.

"I've been feeling like such an outsider the last few days," I admitted.

He lifted my chin and looked into my eyes. "I'm sorry I made you feel that way," he said, drawing me toward him and hugging me hard.

I couldn't help but smile.

Emotionally available. *Check.*

Discovery

While Rick and I dated, I was learning to recognize and address "red flags" and "deal-breakers" as they occurred in our relationship, instead of ignoring and making excuses for them. I made a point of acknowledging issues and communicating my feelings and perceptions about behaviors that made me feel uncomfortable.

Many people who have suffered trauma in their childhood do not have healthy boundaries with themselves or others. For those of us who struggle with this issue, using the rational mind to address real or perceived challenges without falling into old, unhealthy patterns of thinking and acting is essential. By using logic to come to a place of sound resolution and, ultimately, to a place of happiness, I was able to trust that I would make good decisions for myself.

Discretion will protect you, and understanding will guard you.

—PROVERBS 2:11 (NIV)

Just Love Him

Chocolate cake with no frosting. I think that's the best way to describe the way I was feeling about my relationship with Rick.

Several months had passed since Jacob's birth, and Rick and I had settled into a comfortable routine. Every day I became more at ease with his laid-back way. Somehow, though, it all felt a little . . . well, I hate to say the word, but since I'm being honest, I'll admit it: Our relationship felt boring.

Late one afternoon as I chatted with Carlene, she asked, "Is it possible that you're struggling because he's a really good guy?"

I had considered that possibility. My relationship with Rick was very calm, and I wasn't used to it. In the past, I had been attracted to difficult and unpredictable men—men who kept me on pins and needles.

"It's possible," I admitted. "I'm still trying to wrap my mind around my feelings. He and I do such a good job of working things out. We respect each other, we have lots of fun, and we're really attracted to each other, so what else could it be?"

"Maybe you're just not used to being with someone who treats you well?" she asked.

"I hear what you're saying, Carlene, but honestly, the problem is that it feels like there's just no . . ."

Once more I hesitated.

"Shazam?" she asked.

"Maybe that's it," I answered.

"Well, keep in mind that you've said for you, 'shazam' has always been drama," she offered.

"I know," I agreed.

"And you've also said that there's no place for that in your life anymore."

I nodded and once more agreed. "True. I *definitely* don't want that anymore."

Silence hung on the line between us for a few moments before I chuckled and asked, "Is it possible that I'm just a lunatic?"

She burst into laughter when she answered, "Well, we already knew that."

I smiled as I pictured her face pulled into a silly grin.

"Oh, well," I said. "I'm sure I'll work it out."

After chatting for a few more minutes, we ended the call with a cheery promise to talk again soon.

As I thought about my conversation with Carlene, my thoughts flashed back to a night several months earlier when I had returned home to the house Rick and I shared. His truck had been parked in the driveway, but even though it was well after dusk, there were no lights on in the house.

Concerned, I had unloaded the groceries and headed inside. As I entered the vestibule, the vibration of a heavy, pounding bass reverberated through the center of my body. Stepping into the kitchen, I saw only the tiny red and green lights flashing on the stereo in the otherwise-dark living room. The scene felt surreal as the music blared around Rick's shadowy silhouette.

I switched on the kitchen lamp and dropped the groceries on the table as I waved toward him.

"Bad day?" I mouthed over the music. But he turned away, his face somber, his shoulders bent into the sound blasting from the stereo.

Dinner had been quiet, my attempts at conversation met with only a series of nods. By then I knew that he tended to withdraw when he was having a bad day, but that knowledge didn't make it any easier. I have always been all about communication, and it was a difficult adjustment getting used to his occasional bouts of silent brooding. Because we were still getting to know each other, I worried that his brooding might explode into anger at any moment.

The following morning, as I had climbed into my car to head to the office, I sent a prayer up and over the old pine trees that lined our driveway. "God, please help me. I'm trying so hard to figure out if Rick is the right guy for me."

Only moments later, I noticed a small spider on my car's windshield, just above the wiper blade. The impact it had on me was completely unexpected, so when I arrived at my office, I had hurried inside, dropped my purse onto my desk, and without taking off my coat, typed Rick the following email:

Hi, Rick.

I had the most interesting thing happen to me this morning. When I left the house, I noticed there was a very small spider on my windshield. It was still there when I got on the ramp onto the highway, and as I sped up, the little guy crouched down, hanging on with all eight legs. I found myself applauding his tenacity but quickly forgot about him until I began to decelerate on the ramp into town. It was as I slowed down that the spider raised itself up to look around. But then, as I sped up again, it crouched even lower, hanging on for dear life until I arrived at the office. When I stopped in the parking lot, it stood up, looked around, and skittered across the hood and then over the side. So, you're probably wondering why I'm sharing this with you. Well, what I realized as I was walking into the office is that that little spider is kind of a metaphor for life. When the "winds" of bad days and unexpected events blow against us, all we can do is crouch down and hang on tight until the gusts have passed or until we get home, where we should have peace.

A few months ago, I read some research that said the first ten minutes in the house after work sets the tone for the rest of the evening. Last night was a sucky evening.

That's okay; I'm sure we'll have plenty. But I would just as soon cut them off at the pass.

Love, Chrissie

I had been nervous that night when I returned home because his response to my email had seemed terse. "I'm sorry. We'll talk tonight."

As I joined him on the couch, where he sat stroking my cat Trix's head, his expression had been serious. "I loved your email," he said. "At first I thought it was a cute story, but then I felt like a jerk."

"You should have," I agreed, at first matching my expression to his serious one but then flashing him a grateful grin.

"That's fair," he answered, looking relieved. "What I did last night was wrong, and I will do my best to be sure it doesn't happen again. But if it does happen, I want you to call me on it immediately."

I nodded. "Thank you. I will."

As I had headed to the refrigerator to take out the makings of dinner, I said, "Look, Rick, when you've had a bad day, just tell me. I'll stay out of your way if that's what you want. But when you say nothing at all, I get really nervous."

He stepped toward me and wrapped me in one of his warmest hugs. "We have so much good between us," he said.

As I relaxed against his body, I answered, "I think so, too."

"And I want to keep it that way," he said.

229

That had all happened several months earlier, and we had become even more comfortable with each other since then. Sighing inwardly, I thought, *Maybe Carlene is right. Maybe I'm just not used to a really good guy.*

A few weeks later, I entered the house feeling super-excited.

"Rick, I didn't mention this to you because I didn't know if anything would come of it, but I was interviewed by a business magazine a while back."

His eyes smiled as my trembling fingers opened to the center of the magazine I was holding, where several photos were highlighted. With a grin, I pointed to my picture on the top right.

"This is so good!" I said happily, expounding on all the opportunities that would follow from being one of the featured professionals. During dinner, I chattered on about an ongoing challenge with a difficult business partner and about the contract negotiations for the office lease renewal.

I was shocked, and a little indignant, when he stopped me mid-sentence.

"Chrissie, I'd like a new rule in this house," he said.

"Okay," I answered, feeling confused.

"I'd like to keep discussions about work to fifteen minutes a night. There is more to life than work, and I would appreciate a little more balance at home."

With that, he stood up and began clearing the table.

In a flash, it became clear to me that since Rick had spent his career working for a corporation, he didn't have a clue what it was like to be an entrepreneur. If he was going to put a limitation on me talking about my work, this could be a deal-breaker.

Feeling annoyed, I paced the living room while he loaded the dishwasher in the kitchen. After a few minutes, I threw on my coat and headed out the door. For more than an hour, my thoughts ran wild as I walked harder than I had in a long time. But as my body tired, I headed home, where I settled in on the front-porch steps.

With the night chill creeping in around me, I studied the stars in the pitch-black sky. Why couldn't Rick just be happy for me? It was a big deal to be recognized the way I had been, and he hadn't even congratulated me.

But then, if I was to be completely honest with myself, I would have to admit that he wasn't the first person who had suggested I placed an unhealthy emphasis on my work. Carlene and our good friend Marcia had both commented on several occasions about how unbalanced my life seemed to them, as had Gabriel and my boys. Yet each time anyone had broached the topic, I had insisted that they just didn't understand.

Sitting alone in the dark, my hands buried deep in the pockets of my coat, for the very first time I began to wonder if maybe they were right. Maybe *I* was the one who was wrong and it was *me* who didn't understand.

Suddenly I was hit by another thought that caused a feeling of dread to run through me. What if I focused less on my clients and more on my home life with Rick, and then our relationship failed? At least I knew for sure I could count on the security my work offered. Counting on a significant other hadn't worked out so well for me in the past. Was Rick truly different? Only time was going to tell that story. In the meantime, how would I balance my work and my personal life while maintaining a high level of service for my clients?

Just as the wind picked up, another thought hit me. Was I being selfish? A sensation of uncertainty accompanied a sinking feeling in my center, and I shivered. Rick had made many concessions and compromises for the betterment of our relationship, and he was happy to do so. But what about me? I had stamped off in anger when he had suggested we try to have more balance at home.

For a moment, I was embarrassed, but then I reasoned that his words had hit me like he was issuing a directive rather than suggesting an idea that was open for discussion.

For a few minutes I pondered the night sky. It seemed to me that the stars were cutting miniature holes through the darkness and the tiny, twinkling lights were sending me a message of encouragement. I drew in a deep breath and then emptied my lungs with a long, hard sigh. *What would it hurt for me to try it his way for a couple of months?*

The following morning, Rick's uncertain eyes followed me around the kitchen as I prepared my tea, packed a lunch, and got ready to leave. I wanted to reassure him, but I was so confused that I wasn't even sure what I would be reassuring him about.

Before he headed out the door, he bent down and kissed me on the head.

"Have a good day," he said.

I nodded without answering.

Work that day was busy. By the time I was able to leave the office, it was well after six o'clock. As I rushed to my car with my head bent against a powerful wind, a cold rain sliced sideways, chilling me to the bone.

Driving on the dark, slick roads was treacherous, and I was so engrossed in keeping my car on the road that I was surprised when I glanced to the left and noticed the majestic stone grotto that housed a statue of Mother Mary. I hadn't realized I was so close to home. Slowing down, I considered stopping and then shook my head and accelerated. I rarely went to church, and I had never stopped at a statue to pray. But I wasn't ready to go home, so without thinking I turned my car around and pulled into the empty parking area.

As I hurried to the shelter of the grotto, the wind ripped at my coat, slapping it hard against my thighs. With my arms wrapped tightly around my waist, I stepped under the overhanging roof. There was a hush in the small space even with the storm raging just a few feet away. For several minutes, I stood studying the detail of the magnificent gray structure illuminated only by soft blue lights. Slowly my eyes moved up the smooth lines of the carved statue, finally coming to rest on the peaceful face of Mother Mary.

"I don't know what I'm doing here," I whispered. After a few long seconds, I knelt on the damp, cold bench, folded my hands, and bowed my head. Suddenly a sob rose in my throat as I prayed, "Mary, I'm so lost. Rick is everything good and decent that I didn't even know existed in a man, but for some reason, I'm confused. What should I do?"

I barely heard the wind and rain that continued slashing just a few feet away as I remained with my head bowed and my fingers intertwined. Lost in my thoughts, I was startled when a tender and compassionate voice spoke into my ear. "Just love him."

I jumped, my head snapping from right to left. I had lost track of time while I prayed, but I hadn't heard anyone come up behind me. When I looked around it was clear that, other than me, the grotto was completely empty. Even the church next door remained dark, and my car was the only one in the lot. Raising my eyes to the statue's face, I stared up at it. Had I *imagined* the voice?

By then the storm had died down and the phone in my purse indicated that I had been at the grotto for close to an hour. Digging deep into my coat pocket for my keys, I walked to my car, tossing one last glance over my shoulder at the statue.

When I reached home only minutes later, I pulled off my coat and leaned on a chair in the living room.

"I'm sorry I'm late," I said to Rick, who was sitting on the couch with Trix cuddled against his leg.

Drawing in a long, fortifying breath, I prepared myself to be as honest as I could be.

"I think it's time for me to tell you why I've been so quiet," I said. In a torrent, the words tumbled out. I admitted that other important people in my life had also pointed out my lack of balance between work and personal time. I explained my fears about my work not being a primary focus. I acknowledged the doubts that continued to plague me about our relationship, even sharing that sometimes it felt a little boring. Then I confessed my biggest concern.

"Rick, I'm worried that I will end up being a disappointing partner."

After a short pause, I told him about my unplanned visit to the grotto. For a moment, I considered telling him about the voice I'd heard there, but decided against it. He would probably think I was crazy anyway.

When I finally fell silent, he stood up and moved to where I still leaned against the chair. Taking my chin in his hand, he tipped my head back and looked into my eyes.

"It's easy with me, Chrissie. There's no need to worry so much."

With his reassurance, a sense of calm came over me, so I laid my head against his chest. When he bent his head to mine, he whispered, "Just love me."

Discovery

This story is not about "getting the guy." Rather, it is about learning to honor and respect the person I had grown to be. Dating someone who was not my usual type continued to be a learning experience for me. It required that I think and act in a different manner than I was used to. Because I was determined to have a healthy relationship, I focused on being healthy myself by learning to respect my boundaries and distinguishing between what behavior was acceptable to me and what was not. I was also communicating my feelings and perceptions, respecting my own value, and using my rational mind to make better decisions for myself.

What I hadn't expected was that making these changes would cause the process to feel so clinical and flat. Transforming into the person I wanted to be was by no means an easy feat, and it took time for me to feel comfortable with it all.

As our relationship grew, it became evident that I was not used to a partnership where there was minimal drama, and it felt very strange to me. In the past, I had fallen into the familiar and just followed my heart. But with Rick, both my head *and* my heart needed time to adjust to a different way of discerning. By that time, I had come to realize that what I had once believed was passion was really just unnecessary drama.

The "icing on the cake" was experiencing the miracle at the grotto. Hearing what I believe were Mother Mary's words—"Just love him"—and then nearly the same words echoed by Rick less than an hour later—was confirmation that I was on the right path. I was doing the work necessary to value myself, and by doing so, would ultimately honor my relationship with Rick.

It took me some time to truly understand the remarkable nature of the relationship Rick and I were developing. Along the way, I began to realize that the bond we were building was not boring at all. In fact, it was fun, exciting, thought-provoking, stimulating, and just plain wonderful—no drama necessary. Rick and I truly brought out the best in each other. Much like my uncle Neil, Rick is a good, loving, supportive man, possessing the qualities needed to build a healthy relationship.

In time, I became so confident in my abilities of discernment that on October 4, 2014, with Carlene and two of our close friends standing beside me, I married him!

Many are the plans in a person's heart,
but it is the Lord's purpose that prevails.

—PROVERBS 19:21 (NIV)

A Deeper Meaning

Through this discovery process, I was able to unearth the roots of the challenging negative patterns in my life. Doing the work necessary to look this honestly at myself wasn't easy, and there were moments I wanted to give up, but I was determined to stay the course. Interestingly, by the time I finished the last of the stories, I realized that I had uncovered an even deeper and richer meaning—one that finally helped me understand the anxiety that has plagued me for a large part of my life.

As I revealed in the earlier chapters of this book, I was born with a strong sense of a greater power—a Presence that was huge and loving and wanted me to have a beautiful life—a Presence I learned to call God. By the time I was three years old, I had a clear awareness that life was a purposeful event, and I was conscious of a peaceful feeling of love and acceptance in the moments when I felt the Presence closest to me. Even as a very young child, I was grateful to have the opportunity of being brought up on a farm in the country, where I could see and feel this God Presence everywhere around me.

By the time I was seven years old, my faith in a loving God Presence began to be brought into question by my parents and local religious leaders. During that same time, I was being taught both at home and at church that God was judging me and I should fear Him. This angry God only rewarded those who followed the rules of the Catholic Church and did not question its teachings. I also learned that church buildings of other denominations were to be avoided because the people who attended services there did not know the truth that I had been so lucky to be born into. To make it more overwhelming, I had the added responsibility for the souls of my classmates who hadn't been born into the truth. I was responsible for the eternal damnation of their souls if I did not direct them to the correct teachings. For many of my young years, I was terrified for them.

It was around this same time that I began to notice the inconsistencies in my parents' behavior. Our house was filled with tension, and I was often on "pins and needles" just waiting for the next explosive outburst, yet as soon as we arrived at church, my parents offered fellow churchgoers warm handshakes and big smiles. As a result, it was difficult not to be mistrusting of the smiles, hugs, and kindnesses that were extended to us by fellow parishioners. I wanted to believe the people in my church were sincere, but I couldn't help feeling suspicious. By the time I made my First Communion, I began to question my own inner knowing, and it was then that I experienced my first bouts of anxiety. On the day I was asked to leave a religious education class for asking what I thought was a valuable question, I made a decision—I would study, learn, and find the truth out for myself. It was with that decision I became a seeker.

I started my search for the truth in churches. When I married my first husband, I became a member of the Lutheran Church. For many years I was happy there as I enjoyed singing in the choir, teaching in the Sunday School, and holding a place on the church council. I became very good friends with the minister, and he often stopped at my house for tea and long conversations about religion, spirituality, and philosophy. He even started a Bible study group at the church when I confided that I had taken a course in college called *The Bible as Literature* but, other than what I learned in that class, knew very little else about it. What I didn't admit to him was that, at the time, I was also studying the Bible with both the Jehovah's Witnesses and the Mormons and intermittently attending a born-again church.

As my anxiety continued to escalate, I began studying several healing modalities in the hope of finding some relief there. When I was invited to a meditation circle at a small arts and wellness shop near my house, I jumped at the opportunity. I was disappointed, however, when the experience was a complete failure. I struggled to bring my mind to a state of stillness, but as hard as I tried, it continued to run off in at least twenty different directions as soon as it was time to move inward. It was almost as if everything that I didn't have time to think about during the day presented itself as soon as it was time to bring my mind to silence. However, I had several friends who swore by meditation, so I kept at it, and with time and determination I was occasionally able to bring myself to a place of calm.

One Sunday afternoon, I decided I would try meditating on my own. By then I had learned techniques to keep my mind focused, so I perched myself on the couch in my music room with a small stone clutched in my hand that would act as a focal point. During that meditation, I was excited when I received a powerful indication that I was on the path back to the God Presence I had known as a child. With more time and lots of practice, the meditations became increasingly fruitful. In time, my feelings of anxiety lessened and have since then completely gone. From there, it has been one miracle after the other.

One of the most incredible miracles in my life has been my connection with the female energy of Mother Mary. As a child, every Sunday I would study a statue of her that stood just to the left of the altar. Her face was so beautiful and peaceful. But even though her figure was in a place of prominence in our church, I remember very little discussion of her except during the Christmas or Easter season. After experiencing what I believed to be her voice in the grotto that day while I prayed, I began to read everything I could get my hands on about her. The amount of information I uncovered was astounding. I think the most important thing I learned was that she was a powerful woman with great trust in God's plan.

Another miracle has been bringing this book to fruition. Through our combined efforts, Carlene and I worked through the stories and discoveries because we believe we were meant to do this together. We also believe that God has been our guiding force every step of the way. When I was feeling overwhelmed by the amount of inner work necessary to bring this to completion, or when I struggled with finding the right words to convey these sometimes very difficult stories, together we prayed for guidance. In each case, the answers came.

Before now, I have been very uncomfortable talking about my faith in any kind of public way. It has always been my belief that faith is a very personal topic and that each of us experiences it in different ways. So, it was yet another miracle when I suggested that we add Bible verses at the end of each chapter. Imagine my surprise when Carlene handed me a legal pad full of quotes she had already researched. She, too, had felt the call to recognize and praise God's presence in this work, and she was already two steps ahead of me. In several cases when it was more difficult to find the exact verse we were looking for, after sending out a prayer for guidance, the perfect verse and version came through some very unexpected sources.

Now I'm going to ask you to bear with me for a moment while I make what I believe is a very important point. A few years ago, after chatting with a friend who was struggling in her relationship, I found myself scribbling the word *trust,* since it was my sense that trust was the issue she was grappling with. As I stared at the word, though, I began to experience a strange sensation, because I suddenly saw something I had never noticed before. Right in the middle of the word *trust* is yet another word: *us.*

tr-*us*-t

That discovery had such a big impact that it stayed with me and I often thought about it. However, I didn't understand the relevance in my own life until I wrote this book.

I have always loved being in partnerships, whether they are personal or business-related. I believe that, in most cases, two heads are better than one. In a trusted partnership, I feel supported because I believe that my partner has my back. I love the feeling of "us." But I never thought about it as being important in my relationship with God.

For me, faith has never been an issue. I guess you could say I am lucky because even in the worst of times, I never doubted that God existed. What I did come to doubt due to my upbringing, though, was that I could *trust* in God. Early in life, I learned to trust only myself, because I knew that I could rely on me.

Through the course of this discovery process, I came to understand that in the eyes of the child I was at the time, my parents were the personification of God in my life, since they were the center of my universe and held ultimate power over me. Unfortunately, I did not feel I could trust them. As a result, although I continued to believe in the existence of a loving God, by the time I was fourteen I had lost faith that I could trust in Him.

Understanding that I can trust in God—that He and I are in partnership together—is probably the biggest miracle that has come out of this process. Up until this epiphany, I had a good life. I worked hard, loved well, and was good to others, but I was living with a continual underlying fear because I knew I couldn't control my own destiny. What I've learned is that by putting my complete trust in God and viewing God as my *ultimate* partner, anything is possible. I know am safe, and I know that no matter what, I am loved.

Trust in the LORD with all your heart
and lean not on your own understanding.

—Proverbs 3:5 (ESV)

Songbird

A Letter to My Five-Year-Old Self

Dear Chrissie,

I am writing this letter to you from the perspective gained through a lifetime of living, learning, and healing. Before I begin, I want you to imagine that you are at the creek with Uncle Neil, where you are soaking up his unconditional love and acceptance. Feel the warmth of the rock beneath you and the sun on your skin; and let the song of the crickets in the fields beyond be the background music for my words.

You are such a unique little girl, and I'm so proud of you. Everything about you is perfect because, through the miracle of your birth, you are a child of God, which makes you innately lovable, special, worthy, and beautiful.

I love your sensitive soul. Even though you are so young, you feel even the simplest things so deeply. To someone your age, it may feel like a burden, but please believe me when I tell you that it is a gift—a special blessing that in time you will come to understand. It is your sensitivity that will enable you to experience life with compassion and love.

I love your determination and perseverance. You work so hard to shine at whatever you do, no matter how difficult. It is important for you to know that it is okay to release those things that do not bring you happiness. But never let go of your passions. Your love of writing and music will sustain you through the most difficult periods in your life, so continue to hone these skills. Most of all, please know that I will always applaud your efforts, and I will love you regardless of how well you perform.

I love your compassionate and forgiving heart. You accept people for who they are and see the good in them no matter how they present themselves in the world. Your love allows you to meet others where they are in any moment. You shower them with compassion and forgiveness because, even at your age, you recognize that there are no perfect people and that everyone deserves love. In time, you will come to understand that you can maintain your compassion while at the same time guarding your personal boundaries. You will learn that, although it does not feel good, it is healthy for you to feel the pain others inflict on you, because that pain is an indicator that your boundaries have been crossed. Personal boundaries are there to keep you safe, and you will come to recognize that healthy relationships begin with people who understand and respect the importance of this delicate balance.

I love your physical body. You are such a beautiful little girl with your strawberry blonde hair and your blue-green eyes. Your body is healthy and strong, and it will serve you well. Take good care of it, and always treat it with the respect it deserves. Appreciate the benefits it offers you and always view it through kind eyes.

I love your desire for meaningful female friendships. Your craving for close friendships with other females will be a challenging journey for you. It will be one of your most important life lessons. In time, you will learn to be vulnerable and honest with women who truly deserve the honor of your trust because they will accept and love you for who you are.

I love your birth name: Christina. It's such a good name, a strong name—one that fits someone like you. I know that you feel the name is too grand for you because you see it as belonging to someone who is beautiful not only in body but in worth. But you do deserve it. Never doubt that. Did you know that in Latin the name Christina means "follower of Christ"? What a lucky little girl you are to have such an incredible name. I know how much you treasure your nickname of Chrissie because Daddy gave it to you. But one day you will be ready to step into your birth name, and I will be there, applauding you, because you will have worked through so much before you finally feel comfortable using it.

I love your faith in God and your thirst to know the truth. It is yet another gift that you are able to see God in the grass, the flowers, the trees, the insects, and the spiders, as well as in the eyes of the kittens, the cows, and the horses. This allows you the opportunity to appreciate life through a lens of awe and gratitude. Your faith is so sure, but I will tell you that it will be an amazing day when you finally learn to *trust* in God and the plan Spirit has for you.

There is so much more to say, but I will end with this: Never doubt that you came here to sing a very special song. Your song is the one in your heart, the quiet music you hear early in the morning when everyone else is still asleep. Don't hold it inside. Sing it! It is this song that will bring you happiness even on the worst days, because it is your light, the divine light that shines bright within you. And one day you will share your song with the rest of the world, sending a message of vast love, hope, and healing.

So, go ahead and fly, songbird. Be the person you know you came here to be. Soar higher than you can even imagine, for you are truly safe and protected in the arms of the Divine Spirit.

With so much love to you from your older self, I am,
Christina

Blossoms appear in the land. The time of the songbird has arrived.

—SONG OF SOLOMON 2:12 (GW)

A Thoughtful Walk to Forgiveness

When the editors came back with a list of questions after reviewing the manuscript that became this book, the most burning one was about my adult relationships with my parents. I thought it was an excellent point, and I hope what follows answers any questions you may have as well.

My relationship with my mom was neither difficult nor easy because I had always viewed her as someone with whom I was familiar rather than as someone with whom I had a loving, spiritual-like connection. I was curious about her in a more detached sort of way, and when I was young I obviously bowed to her authority over me. As an adult, I understood that my mom and I were very different people who had little in common. Our relationship did not develop any further.

I would like to share what I believe is a remarkable story about the two of us. My mom was diagnosed with Alzheimer's disease when she was in her mid-seventies. My dad took amazing care of her and insisted on doing it all himself, without the help of family or specialized caregivers. As my mom's disease progressed, the memories of us were erased, and one by one we disappeared from her mind.

Several years later, on the day Rick and I got married, my dad arrived at our wedding with my mother on his arm. By then, she no longer resembled the woman she used to be, except for her red hair and bright blue eyes. During the previous year, my dad had been insisting that she often asked for me, but the idea that she would remember *me*, out of all my brothers and sisters, seemed absurd.

That day, though, when the ceremony ended, I took Rick's hand and we moved to my parents' table. My dad immediately said, "Hey, Rosita, here's your daughter Chrissie."

My mother's eyes searched my face for just a moment before she moved forward and wrapped her arms tight around my waist. Leaning her head against my shoulder, she began to repeat over and over, "Thank you, Chrissie." I had the strongest sense that she was thanking me for never judging her. She died nine months later at the age of eighty-six.

My relationship with my dad has been a more difficult and complicated one. As far back as I can remember, I have always loved him so much. He was outgoing, charming, and intelligent, and had great drive and motivation.

As I matured, I began to realize that my dad never stopped moving. I was used to it when I was a kid living at home, and it made sense because there was so much to do. But after being away for several years and then returning home for family events, the behavior struck me as odd. He rarely sat still long enough to have much of a conversation, and I sometimes wondered if my dad was *afraid* of a meaningful personal connection with me. Even if we did begin what seemed like a good exchange, he would usually stop me in the middle of a sentence with an announcement that there was some chore he needed to take care of. Usually, after completing the task, he didn't return to our conversation but instead kept himself busy some other way.

When my father was diagnosed with bone cancer, my confused feelings about our relationship prompted the first stories for this book. I remember waking up in tears one morning only days after I received the news about his illness. I couldn't seem to stop crying no matter how I tried to distract myself. Rick suggested that I was preparing myself for my dad's death, but I knew differently.

As a child, I had always craved a closer connection with my dad. However, it wasn't until my friends married and their fathers walked them down the aisle, planting a kiss on their cheek and crying during the father-daughter dance, that I realized the brokenness of our relationship.

When I married the first time, I walked down the aisle alone because my mother and father chose not to attend. When I married the second time, there was never even a discussion about my father giving me away. Then, when I married Rick, my girlfriends were the ones who sent me off into Rick's arms.

Of course, I immediately forgave my dad each time for the hurt he had caused me because it was my pattern to jump to forgiveness as a quick way to bypass the pain.

But with the diagnosis of my dad's cancer, it became clear to me that I was not getting ready to grieve over his death. I was grieving over what I felt I had missed out on in life, which is a loving father-daughter relationship. For the very first time, I was allowing myself to feel the pain of the loss.

When I thought about my dad's disease more, I found it interesting that the cancer was attacking what might be equated to the trunk of a tree—the solid framework of his physical body. At first, I wondered if the illness was partially due to his carrying the weight of my mother, who required all his attention during the many years she suffered the effects of Alzheimer's disease. It also occurred to me that maybe whatever fueled his constant movement was playing a part. I know from personal experience that if we do not face the things in life that have caused us pain, or if we find a way to convince ourselves that they are not important, our bodies eventually break down under the continued stress.

About twenty years ago, I wrote my dad a letter as part of my birthday gift to him. In the letter, I shared the warm memories that I had held close to my heart since I was a little girl. By pouring out my heart, I had hoped to spark a conversation and, with that, the chance to repair our relationship. When my dad read the letter, he hugged me hard and cried as he thanked me for what I had said. But still the connection I hoped for didn't come, and after a while I finally stopped trying.

When I finished this book, though, I was conflicted. I longed to talk to my dad about what I had discovered through the process, yet at the same time I didn't want to upset him. After all, he was ninety years old and suffering from bone cancer. Ultimately, the decision was taken out of my hands when the publisher requested a letter of permission to publish from my dad. As we sat across from each other in the well-used living room chairs, for the first time in my life I was completely honest with him about my feelings regarding his behavior when I was a child. I explained my discovery process and the understanding gained from it while at the same time reassuring him that I held nothing but forgiveness and compassion in my heart for both him and my mother.

When I finished speaking he asked a few questions, but then he became quiet. A couple of hours later as I sat chatting at the kitchen table with my brother, my dad joined us, sitting down next to me. It was then that he admitted he was aware that his behavior had been unpredictable. Imagine my surprise when he revealed that he had been diagnosed with post-traumatic stress disorder (PTSD) as a result of his years in the military. When I researched the disorder to gain a deeper understanding, I discovered that it was not recognized by the American Psychiatric Association (APA) as a mental disorder until 1980. By that time, I was an adult.

To be clear, I am not saying that the diagnosis of PTSD excuses my dad's behavior. My parents made choices about the way we were raised, and they supported each other in those choices. Nevertheless, this information aided my understanding of his behavior, and it allowed me for the first time since I was a little girl to hug him with complete love and compassion.

At this point, you may be wondering how I feel about everything I uncovered while writing this book. When someone suggested recently that my life had been ruined by my childhood experiences, I burst out laughing. I've had an incredibly interesting life, in part *because* of my childhood. I've traveled all over the globe; I've experienced powerful love and life-changing hurts; and I've had an opening to Spirit that has allowed me to learn that I can trust in a greater plan. I have two amazing boys who have matured into wonderful men, and they have chosen the most incredible women as their mates. Rick's family members have welcomed me into their loving, close-knit group, and I am at peace. I can't imagine having a better life.

One of the most important things I have come to understand as I worked through my relationships with my parents is that it was important for me to first *acknowledge* the pain I had always deflected. It wasn't easy at the beginning to be honest about what had happened or how the events that hurt me had impacted the course of my life. However, once I accepted the truth, I was finally able to work through my feelings.

Another important lesson I have learned through examining my relationships with my parents is to recognize when my boundaries are being crossed. Jumping to forgiveness without first feeling the pain inflicted has been damaging for me on many levels.

Today, pain is my indicator. I have come to realize that allowing myself to feel my pain makes the act of forgiveness more difficult, but it also makes my forgiveness more heartfelt. Forgiving is now a *choice* I make, and it is no longer my automatic response. I have come to understand that when I allow myself to feel pain and I make the choice to forgive, it is an incredible gift—not only to the other person I am forgiving, but also to myself.

Create in me a pure heart, O God, and renew a
steadfast spirit within me.

—Psalm 51:10 (NIV)

Part Three

Love as a Legacy

This next section is laid out in two parts. First, you have the opportunity to consider some of your own childhood memories. The next few pages are prompts intended to spark your thinking. Is there anything that comes up as a repeating thought or pattern that could be rooted in your childhood? If so, the following questions may help you consider a new perspective.

Second, you will have an opportunity to participate in the *I Love My Life Challenge*. To build a legacy of love, you need to love your life. If your current circumstances could use some help, this section will spur you along a path and get you moving in a more positive direction. If you already love your life, I am so happy for you! There are some interesting thoughts to consider that may help you love it even more.

My goal in sharing my stories has been to spark a larger conversation about how changing your perspective can literally change your life. No one is perfect, and that includes parents or caregivers.

Let's begin by contemplating some key ideas, below. Following each section is a series of simple questions meant to start you thinking about your own experiences in a way that may not have occurred to you before. I have left space for you to make notes, but you may find a journal is a more-effective way to track your thoughts.

You as the Primary Love-Giver

As a person of influence in a young person's life, your actions and words are of the highest importance. Whether you are a parent, grandparent, family member, teacher, coach, or so on, it is through a young person's relationship with you that they learn to trust, manage their emotions, determine their personal value, and interact with the world. Because none of us is perfect, in a moment of exhaustion or frustration it is possible to say or do something that may wound a child. In some cases, those words or actions may take a lifetime to undo.

That idea may seem a little overwhelming, but keep in mind that even the *smallest* demonstrations of kindness and love can make a lasting positive difference for a child. In my case, the words of Uncle Neil and my third-grade teacher impacted my life for the better. Just imagine if *you* could be that person for even one child.

- *Did you feel loved and accepted as a child?*

- *Why did you feel that way?*

_____

_____

_____

_____

_____

_____

Love Your Children; Love All Children

I have always appreciated the adage "It takes a village to raise a child." I believe the more genuine and meaningful our relationships are with young people, whether they are family members or not, the more influence we have in shaping the adults they are to become. Young people will work to attain their highest potential when they know an adult believes in them and loves them.

- *As a child, did the members of your community have an influence on you?*

- *Was there any one person who had a special influence on you?*

_____

_____

_____

_____

_____

_____

_____

Love and Quality Time

Think back for a moment to when you were a kid and you had the opportunity to spend some individual time with a parent, a favorite aunt or uncle, or another adult with whom you enjoyed spending time. I can still remember even the smallest detail about the one-on-one time I spent with my uncle. Spending quality time with the young people in your life is an invaluable gift not only to the child but to you as well. Time spent together doing the simple things can build a strong bond between the two of you. It is during these special times that you can really get to know the small but important defining qualities of the young person. Listening closely with no distractions can allow you the space to gain insight into feelings and emotions that might not otherwise be obvious. Young people crave your attention. By making time for individual attention, you are showing that you are there for them. Carving time out of a busy schedule can be challenging, but by offering a young person *quality* time—free from the distractions of handheld devices, siblings, and other influences—you can both benefit.

- *Did you receive quality one-on-one time as a child?*

• *If so, is there a particular day or event that sticks out in your mind?*

_____

_____

_____

_____

_____

_____

Teaching Love by Example

Young people are natural imitators. How many times have you seen a little boy following behind his dad holding a screwdriver or a hammer? How about a little girl applying her mother's lipstick or trying to walk in her mother's high-heeled shoes? I think it's important to keep in mind that teaching by example is the most valuable kind of instruction. The practice of "Do as I say, not as I do" can be confusing, and it sends a contradictory message that may eventually lead to a lack of trust. Of course, none of us is perfect, so when we inevitably fall short, learning from our mistakes and making better choices the next time sends the message that mistakes are normal and that we can recover from them.

• *Did you feel your caregivers were positive role models for you?*

• *Did you learn from their examples?*

• *Did your caregivers send contradictory messages?*

_____

_____

_____

_____

_____

_____

Love in the Praise and Positive Reinforcement

Praise and positive reinforcement can be powerful motivators. Praise feels fantastic because it's validating. Think about the last time somebody said something to you that made you feel appreciated. Take a few seconds and savor that feeling again. It feels amazing, doesn't it?

Regrettably, as human beings, we tend to react more strongly to, and remember, the negative comments we hear more than we do the comparable good ones. Research into "negativity bias" shows that it takes at least five positive statements to repair the damage of one harmful one. So it's important that when we need to reprimand a young person, we do it in a positive way rather than focusing on his or her weakness or deficiency. Starting or finishing a correcting statement using demeaning words is not good, nor is it necessary.

• *Did you receive praise and positive reinforcement as a young person?*

- *Did it come from your family? Community members? Teachers?*

- *Who praised you the most?*

- *How did that praise or positive reinforcement make you feel about yourself?*

- *Did an adult make negative comments to you or about you?*

_____

_____

_____

_____

_____

_____

Love Has No Labels

According to *Webster's Dictionary*, the definition of the word *quality* is "a distinctive characteristic." When a young person understands that he or she possesses a certain characteristic or quality, an entire world of possibilities may open up. A child who is athletic may become a baseball player or a soccer player, and a child with a nice voice may aspire to be a singer or a speaker.

On the other hand, a *label* is defined as "a classification," which is by nature limiting. Labels can rigidly define a young person to the exclusion of the other distinctive qualities that are uniquely his or hers, and they can decrease a young person's ability and desire to explore other interests.

Many young people will work to live up to the labels that have been assigned to them. Consider for a moment a young person you've known in your lifetime who was labeled as "trouble," or, conversely, as a "good kid." Did that young person live up to that label?

- *Were you assigned a label as a child?*

- *What was that label?*

- *Do you feel the label limited your potential?*

- *Did you live up to the assigned label, or did you choose a different path?*

- *Were you aware of your special qualities as a child?*

- *What are your special qualities?*

- *How have these special qualities affected your life?*

_____

_____

_____

_____

_____

_____

_____

Love Lives in the Stillness

I don't think there is anything more wonderful in life than lying in the grass and staring at the clouds overhead while listening to the birds sing. Feeling the breeze on my face and the grass against the backs of my legs brings me fully into the moment. Doing this for even a very short time can be refreshing, as it fills a place inside me that longs for quiet.

Our culture continues to evolve into one of hyperstimulation in which marketers bombard us with constant messages. As a society, we have become so used to the constant distraction of social media and the easy availability of online entertainment that many of us have become bored in the silence. Unfortunately, this constant overstimulation can sap our energy, which adds to the stress of daily life and slowly diminishes the *quality* of life.

There are many wonderful benefits to establishing periods of quiet and stillness not only in our own daily routines but also in the routines of our young people. Within the quiet is a state of awareness that can enhance our ability not only to listen, but to hear. It brings us fully into the moment, boosts our mental clarity, and enhances our focus. From this place of awareness, self-discovery can lead to new levels of creativity.

- *Was there a practice of stillness in your house as a child?*

• *How could you make stillness an "activity" for your family?*

• *How can you make it part of your daily routine?*

_____

_____

_____

_____

_____

_____

Love and the Mind–Body Connection

I have no doubt that the human body responds to the way we think, feel, and act—especially since my experience with being "On My Knees." I still have the double vision to prove just how powerful the mind–body connection can be.

Now consider your own experience. Think about the last time you were feeling anxious or worried. Did your heart race? Maybe you developed a rash or bit your fingernails. Poor emotional health can affect our physical, mental, and spiritual health, making it difficult for us to stay grounded, peaceful, happy, and loving.

Young people may not be equipped to understand the feelings that are invoked by headlines or by upsetting events in the household. When they are confused by their feelings, it is our job to help them identify what is bothering them. Encouraging them to talk about their feelings can help them understand what they are experiencing. Supporting a young person in learning to live an emotionally balanced life is a gift that can last a lifetime.

- *Did you feel encouraged to voice your worries and fears as a child?*

- *If so, how did that make you feel?*

_____

_____

_____

_____

_____

_____

Encouraging Love through Spirituality

Spirituality means many different things to people because our spiritual journeys are so personal. For many, spirituality may be worshipping through organized religion, while others find truth and peace by spending time in nature. Still others practice spirituality by donating their time and services or regularly practicing gratitude. All teachings based in love, forgiveness, compassion, grace, humility, kindness, and respect can offer a firm foundation for spiritual growth.

- *As a child, did you question your spirituality, including your purpose here on Earth?*

- *What kinds of questions did you have?*

_____

_____

_____

_____

_____

_____

Love and Forgiveness

Forgiveness can be thought of as a conscious, deliberate decision to release feelings of resentment or vengeance toward a person or group who has caused harm. It took me some time to understand and appreciate that forgiving someone who I felt had hurt me does not mean that I have glossed over or excused the offending behavior or event. Instead, forgiveness offers the power to release feelings of frustration or anger rather than allowing them to cause ongoing negativity that, in the long run, will only hurt *me*. Forgiveness is a choice—one that leads to healing and, ultimately, to a place of peace.

- *Was your childhood home a place of forgiveness?*

- *Why do you feel that way?*

_____

_____

_____

_____

_____

_____

_____

Love as Your *Legacy*

Becoming a parent or a love-giver is an enormous responsibility for which few of us have been trained. To make it even more challenging, if we have more than one child, we quickly discover that every child is different—so different, in fact, that each may need to be nurtured in an entirely different way.

As I worked my way through this discovery process, uncovering wounds that had been buried for years, it became clear to me that the biggest gift (legacy) I can give the young people in my life is to get healthy myself.

As parents, we begin planning for our children's future before they're born, saving money for college or starting an investment program. But I have come to understand that there is no legacy more important than a legacy of love—one that can be born through our own healing process. When we are finally able to identify the source of our pain, we can heal the wounds that have caused damaging behaviors. When the harmful pattern that may have been passed down from generation to generation is broken, our children do not suffer. What an extraordinary gift to leave the young people in our lives!

You have an opportunity to start your own 3 Rs path! Read on and get ready to start changing your life for the better.

A healthy tree cannot bear bad fruit, nor can a diseased tree bear good fruit.

—MATTHEW 7:18 (ESV)

The I Love My Life Challenge

You can't go back and change the beginning, but you can start where you are and change the ending.

—C. S. LEWIS

Since transforming my life through the 3Rs path (Reveal, Release, Reclaim), I am passionate about helping others along their journey toward personal growth. I have worked with both groups and individuals to develop this guidebook, so I sincerely hope you will find it valuable.

In this chapter, I first offer you some concepts that helped me along my own path. In some cases, I share stories to clarify more-complex ideas. I have also included graphics for those who are visual learners.

Then, it's your turn. Please bear in mind that this is not intended to be a quick fix. Instead, it is a challenge meant to jump-start you on the 3Rs path.

The *I Love My Life Challenge* started during some of the darkest moments of my life. My heart was broken. To make things worse, my professional life was at a crossroad because the work that I had done for years no longer brought me joy. This "perfect storm" caused my anxiety and self-doubt to soar. There were times when my future appeared so bleak I could barely breathe. For the first time ever, my usual positive attitude was literally nonexistent.

Thankfully, a friend who is also a life coach suggested an exercise she believed would be helpful. I was to write *I Love My Life* in bold marker on 3x5 cards and post them around my house and office. The idea was that each time I saw a card I would say, "I love my life" out loud in a clear, confident voice. Considering the state of my emotions at the time, the idea seemed ludicrous, so honestly, it took another few months before I was desperate enough to try.

But one night, after a particularly difficult conversation with my son, I grabbed a stack of 3x5 cards, sat myself at the kitchen table, and got to work. Upon finishing a dozen cards, I made my way through the house, planting them in strategic locations. I put one on my nightstand, one on the bathroom mirror, one on the refrigerator door, one on the door to the cellar, and yet another on the door to the deck. Then, I went to my home office where I added one to my computer screen, another to the filing cabinet, and still another on the door itself. Because my work included lots of driving, I went to the garage to add another to the dashboard of my car. As I reentered the house, I taped one on the garage door and another on the banister. The last one ended up on the television screen in the living room.

Upon waking the following morning, I picked up the card I had placed on my nightstand the night before. Although it had seemed like a good idea the night before, as I stared at the card I felt my stomach clenching into a tight knot. Who was I kidding? I didn't love my life. I didn't even like it. Was trying to convince myself really going to help? I tapped the card against my leg before laying it back on the stand. As I sat staring out the window, though, a small voice in the back of my head asked, *What would it hurt to try?*

I will admit that my voice didn't sound too convincing, but I gave myself credit for the attempt. Maybe I didn't love my life right now, but in the past, it had been good. I believed in the power of positivity. When I thought about it, I understood that everything had begun going downhill when I'd adopted the behavior of feeling sorry for myself. By focusing on the negative, I allowed self-doubt to get the best of me. The only thing in life I could control was my attitude, and that would come when I maintained control of my thoughts.

With that realization, the course I had been on for a couple of years began to change direction.

Throughout the day, and for the weeks and months that followed, I continued to declare, "I love my life" multiple times every day.

Things began to look up within just a few days. I noticed I was smiling more. I also noticed that instead of placing the lion's share of my focus each day on the not-so-great circumstances in my daily life, I was counting my wins—the little things each day that brought me enjoyment. For example, instead of considering walking my dog during the rainy month of April as another chore, I consciously stopped several times during each outing to breathe in fresh air and listen to the sound of the rain meeting the leaves. At night as I went to bed, I savored the sound of my cat's purr as he settled next to my pillow.

Quickly, I resumed my hobby of songwriting. I began making more time for my friends and family, which diminished my feelings of isolation. When I decided to release a difficult client, one who expected lots of attention but who resisted paying the bill, a new, more-lucrative account materialized within a week. As I started to feel happier, everything became easier.

I realized that the key was to focus on catching my negative thoughts. I paired this with counting and recording any small win in each day. Plus, I asked myself lots of very hard questions and answered myself as honestly as possible. Within a year, I had a full roster of great clients, I was once more performing at local clubs and coffeehouses, and I treated myself to a week away in Northern California. When friends and colleagues asked me how I'd risen out of my funk, I answered that I had simply changed my mind.

The *I Love My Life Challenge* was a first giant step in healing through the 3Rs. As time went on and I gained more clarity (Reveal), the anxiety and self-doubt that had plagued me throughout my life became nearly nonexistent because I had liberated myself (Release). The new level of self-confidence gained provided the courage to overcome my fear of public speaking (Reclaim). By then I'd become passionate about sharing what I had learned, and therefore, more determined to speak to whoever would listen. Before long, I was presenting at both private and corporate events, which added to my confidence.

At every presentation, without fail, I was asked why some childhood memories leave such a strong impression and how my listeners could detach themselves from the effects of those experiences. By then, I had been studying the work of several noted neuroscientists for a couple of years. One of the most fascinating things I learned early on is from the work of Dr. Bruce Perry, author of *The Boy Who Was Raised as a Dog*. He explains that as a child, your brain operates much like a sponge, soaking up the words and actions of the adults in your life. You imitate what you see, but more importantly, your brain is busy cataloging what it needs to do to keep you safe. As a result, thought and behavior patterns are being ingrained—in many cases, without your knowledge. Perry also explains that by the time you are seven years old, many of the behavior patterns that will play a large role in your life as an adult are already in place.

This idea might be a bit disconcerting, so thank goodness for the work of such noted neuroscientists as Dr. Caroline Leaf. Author of *Switch on Your Brain*, Dr. Leaf speaks to the miracle of *neuroplasticity*. She describes the brain as being "plastic," and therefore malleable. The beauty of neuroplasticity is that by making a practice of catching your negative thoughts and then positively redirecting them, you can literally rewire your brain to be more positive. With this change, your new healthier thought patterns lead you to healthier behaviors. My story is a perfect example of neuroplasticity in action.

While researching, I discovered neuro-linguistics programming (NLP), first made popular by Richard Bandler and John Grinder in the late 1970s. NLP is not a science; rather, it is a body of concepts and ideas like those Carlene and I used to get to the root of my issues. Since NLP concepts changed the course of my life by opening my eyes and mind to a new perspective, I use it in my work with both groups and individuals. It is so much fun to see people change and grow using this method.

What is NLP?

In its most simplistic form, neuro-linguistics programming is a way of retraining your brain. The popularity of NLP has become widespread since it was first introduced in the 1970s. Since then it has been used as a way to identify the thought and behavior patterns of successful individuals and teach them to others. The success of NLP has been life-changing. By retraining your brain to understand past experiences through a different perspective, you learn to embrace possibility in a way you may never have imagined.

Core concepts

The core concepts of NLP that I focus on in my work are as follows:

1) *Generally, people respond to perception rather than reality.*
The fact is that you witness the world based on your past experiences. Those experiences feed your perception. In other words,

what happened to you in the past is the foundation of your opinion today. As life progressed, you gained a set of understandings. Those beliefs influence your thoughts about yourself and your world.

Let's say, for instance, that you are struggling with self-doubt. As you have witnessed through my stories and ensuing discoveries, it is possible that the root of your self-doubt can be traced to your child-hood. Thanks to the gift of neuroplasticity, by digging in to understand the truth of your past experiences, you begin owning your personal power, which allows you to step confidently into your life's purpose.

2) *Feelings are not facts.*
Your emotions are powerful because they are fueled by the energy produced by negative thoughts. But simply because you *feel* a certain way does not mean that what you are feeling is the truth. For instance, take a moment to recall something that happened that upset you. How did you feel? Was there any time you can remember when you were upset and found out later that your initial thoughts were incorrect? By looking at the source of your emotion, you gift yourself the possibility of seeing things from a more helpful and hopeful point of view.

3) *Personal responsibility equals personal empowerment.*
When you take responsibility for your thoughts, behaviors, mis-takes, and/or career path, you gain self-confidence. With greater self-confidence you have a greater sense of personal power. For example, has there ever been a time in your life when you apol-ogized for something you did that hurt another? How was your

apology received? How did you feel when you were forgiven? Taking responsibility builds self-confidence, and from that place, you are off and running toward a life you love.

4) *Everything is achievable.*
This idea that everything is achievable may initially sound like a tall tale. But when you set yourself a goal, you can bring it to fruition by outlining the small stepping-stones necessary to get where you want to go. By asking yourself what it will take to reach your goal, you are able to break down your plan into small manageable tasks. Doing so will help you to easily measure your small successes, which in time will bring you to your big goal. Keep in mind that it is essential to celebrate each little win, *no matter how small*. Each small success takes you one step closer to a life you love.

Before You Continue

You are about to embark on a path of personal change. To get yourself started, take a moment to write *I Love My Life* on 3x5 cards or some other medium. If you prefer, you can get creative. Paint it on your wall! Post colorful sheets of paper around your space! Take a picture and use it as the wallpaper for your phone and laptop! For this to work, it is crucial that the message be front and center where it can act as a constant reminder. If you own a car, and especially if you drive a lot, be sure you post your reminder there as well. The idea is to make this a daily practice that you work on all day, every day.

Please don't skip this step! By placing multiple reminders that you see repeatedly, you are taking personal responsibility for your own success. Go ahead and do it now. It is too important a piece of the puzzle to put off.

What do you desire?

Before you get started, you will want to gain some understanding on a few important points. The tools below will help you identify any possible roadblocks.

What is holding you back?

Let's say your big vision is to leave your nine-to-five job to start your own business. You have wanted to start a business for years, but your brain is screaming that you have bills to pay, children to feed, and tuition payments coming due. Starting a business is out of the realm of possibility.

If any of these types of thoughts blast into your brain, congratulations! You are experiencing the effects of the *negativity bias.* Because your brain is programmed to protect you, this is its way of preparing you for the worst. It is warning you of all the dangers involved with a significant change in your life. What if you lose your money, or worse, your family or friends? What if your big dream does not work out? What will you do then?

The negativity bias is an especially important concept to understand. Science has proven that human beings are wired to register negativity more quickly than anything positive. We are also wired to dwell on negative experiences.

Here's an example: You arrive at your resort hotel after a long trip. You are delighted when the representative at the front desk offers you an upgrade at no charge. Then, the bellhop shares the name of his favorite restaurant where he promises an exquisite meal for an inexpensive price. As you unpack your bags and hang up your clothes, you notice the bottle of wine chilling in the cooler. You pull on the comfy robe left for you in the closet and head to the bathroom. That's when you see it—a big, black, hairy spider crawling in the sink. Chances are, thanks to your negativity bias and the specially wired trait of dwelling on negative experiences, when you recount the tale to your friends, your story will revolve around the spider rather than the beauty of your surroundings and the kindness of the staff.

To balance the negativity bias, you also have an *optimism bias*. Some theorists believe the optimism bias is a negative thing because they believe people have made crazy choices based on optimism. But this bias is incredibly helpful because it increases your feeling of well-being by offering you optimism about the future.

Understanding how both the negativity bias and the optimism bias are impacting your thoughts will help you more easily assess your plan from a grounded and balanced place.

Starting Your "I Love My Life" Plan

Before launching any plan, it is a good idea to assess your overall well-being. Because our human system is comprised of what I call the *System of Four*—physical, mental, emotional, and spiritual (which includes not only your connection to a higher power, but also to the planet and your environment)—you want to be sure you are balanced with all four. Being balanced produces feelings of confidence.

A few years ago, I launched Let My Legacy Be Love. I made a significant investment to work with several professionals I believed could help me. I was focused, happy, and I could not wait to get to work each day.

But then one morning I woke up with the flu. I was nauseous, feverish, and had a cough that wrenched my body and raked at my swollen throat. I had not been that sick in years.

As I lay there in my bed, unable to sleep and feeling sick as a dog, I began experiencing feelings of self-doubt. Who was I kidding? How could I possibly be helpful to anyone else when I was such a mess myself? Then, I remember glancing at the clock and thinking that I needed a drink but didn't feel well enough to get up. My emotions suddenly flipped from self-doubt to gloom. My husband, Rick, was in the other room reading. When was the last time he had come in to see if I needed anything? Then, a memory of my dog, Hannah, who had passed a year earlier, flashed into my mind. This thought was the final straw that sent me into a full-blown pity party.

Interestingly, though, a few days later when I was physically better, I was right back to feeling excited and optimistic. Aha! This moment birthed the graphic below, which is intended to demonstrate what can happen when your *System of Four* is out of balance. Due to physical illness, I was mentally weaker as well. Without mental strength to catch those nasty negative thoughts, the negativity produced became the energy that fueled my emotions. From there, I succumbed to feelings of misery.

During my programs, people often chant, *I am stable on the table!* I have been told that doing so acts as a reminder that when one "leg" is temporarily weak, self-doubt and uncertainty can creep in.

Measuring your well-being

Understanding and measuring your well-being is exceptionally helpful. Since it is not something that you generally do on a regular basis, a tool I find helpful to assess personal well-being is a word compass. The word compass is intended to help you measure your overall well-being right now. (This tool can be used any time to check in with yourself.)

Physical

Sick Overweight

High Blood Pressure

Skin Issues High Cholesterol

Chronic Pain

Energetic

Flexible Vibrant

Healthy Vital

Mental

Negative Thoughts

Mental Chatter

Indecisive Overwhelmed

Distracted

Positive Thinking Focused

Decisive Steadfast

Creative

Resolute

Emotional

Explosive Distraught

Heartbroken Sad Angry

Isolated Abandoned Empty

Peaceful Content Happy

Grounded Feel Safe

Spiritual

Isolated Abandoned Empty

Forlorn Neglected Lost

Supported Close Loved

Appreciated Seen Heard

The compass is intended to guide you toward a deeper understanding of your *System of Four*. As you are working through the compass, you may notice a physical issue or a mental or emotional pattern which could act as a distraction and therefore become a roadblock on your path to a life you love. The knowledge gained by this exercise offers you the opportunity to address this issue and begin taking charge. Doing so engenders a deeper sense of personal control, which in turn builds self-confidence. The compass is a great tool for catching issues before they can get in the way of your success.

Understanding your mind

I don't think there is anything more fascinating than the human mind. You experience the world differently than anyone else anywhere on Earth. Your perspective, which is your individual point of view, is unique. For this reason, it is crucial to your personal growth process to understand how your individual mind works.

It is a generally accepted idea that there are three types of minds. Each of us is stronger in one than the other. The three types are:

- rational
- emotional
- wise

The **rational mind** considers and guides sensible or logical action. There is no emotion or bias when making a judgment.

The **emotional mind** is the opposite of the rational mind because it does not rely on logic or reason. Instead, it is governed by your moods and what is happening around you in any given moment.

The **wise mind** is the rational mind and the emotional mind working together. The wise mind considers both logic and emotions, yet it is practical, and sensitive to how you feel in any situation. It allows you to see the whole picture. By doing so, you think and act in ways that are not only reasonable, but also authentic to you and your nature. The goal of self-growth is to achieve the wise mind as your dominant force, because it will allow you a clearer vision of every situation.

Below is a graphic that illustrates all three minds. Take a moment to understand which mind is dominant for you. As time goes by, you will notice a change, so this chart is worth revisiting over the years. As you grow and change, you will develop a stronger wise mind. It will be fun for you to watch your own development.

Rational

Intellectual Logical   Facts and Research
Focused   Structured

Emotional

Free Spirit   Emotionally Led
Impulsive Passionate   Reactive

Wise

Balanced Intuitive Sensitive

Aware   Wise

Perception vs. truth

As humans, we generally react to our perceptions. It is a rare person who clearly sees the truth in an emotional moment. The following story illustrates and acts as a reminder that even though a situation may appear to be one thing, there is a possibility that it is in truth something else entirely.

There is a man on a train traveling with two children. It's five o'clock in the evening, so the train is packed with tired businesspeople commuting home from work. The man traveling with his kids is slumped in his seat, flipping through his phone, seemingly oblivious as his kids run up and down the aisle. When the kids push through the crowds, the travelers shoot each other expressions of annoyance.

Finally, a woman leans over, taps the man on the shoulder, and points in the direction of the children. The man looks up and, appearing embarrassed, apologizes to the woman and calls the children back to their seats. Within minutes, though, the kids are running up and down the aisles again while he stares out the window. This time a businessman with a severe expression confronts the man.

"Hey, buddy. You need to get your kids under control."

Once more, the first man looks up, embarrassed. As he gathers the kids toward him, he says, "I'm so sorry. I'm not usually like this. My wife was killed in a car accident a few days ago, and I am not myself. Please forgive me."

The *perception* of the commuters was that the man was a disinterested father who did not discipline his unruly children. The *truth* was that the man was brokenhearted, distraught, and therefore distracted.

I love this example because I think it clearly illustrates how you might view a situation one way while being completely oblivious to the truth of the matter.

Has there been a time when you made a judgment and found out later that you were totally off-base? Take a moment to make a note of your experience. Doing so can help you solidify this concept in your mind.

_____

_____

_____

_____

_____

_____

_____

Our relative world

Years ago, I was shopping when I found a piece of wall art that said *Comparison is the thief of joy.* I recall experiencing a flash of truth, because only seconds earlier, I had been feeling short and unattractive while standing next to my tall and willowy friend.

I believe comparing ourselves to others is natural because we live in a world where everything is relative. Your mind registers short versus tall, dark-skinned versus light-skinned, thin versus heavy. You may find tall people with dark hair and brown eyes more attractive while others prefer blond hair and blue eyes. But it goes much further than mere appearances. For instance, you may believe you are analytical until you spend time with a financial analyst!

An example of comparison stealing joy may be playing center stage in your career. Let's say you love your job and are happy with your pay grade. You are making plenty of money to pay your bills and you have saved enough for a nice vacation during the summer. You feel good about yourself—until your friend gets a promotion with a significant salary upgrade. Suddenly, you begin to feel disgruntled.

Challenging your thoughts

Because you are being inundated all day long with marketing messages, news stories, and other people's thoughts and opinions, you may find yourself comparing what you look like or what you have to others. When these thoughts lead to feelings of insecurity and not-good-enough, it is valuable—if not crucial—to challenge the validity of your thoughts. By challenging them, you begin building more trust in your abilities. Plus, challenging your thoughts raises your self-awareness.

Imagine that you are experiencing a feeling of insecurity. What do you do? You can either allow yourself to feel anxious, or you can challenge the thought that fueled the feeling. Taking charge brings you back into control. With regular practice, you will learn to see thoughts as something outside of yourself. As you become better at gaining control over your thoughts, you will notice it is a three-step process. For instance:

- I notice that I am having a thought.
- The thought I am having is . . .
- I am not good enough."

The graphic below can help you visualize this idea.

Your turn!

Now it is your turn. Get excited! The time is now for you to begin building the foundation of a life that sends you jumping out of

bed each day. The tools on the previous pages will help you identify roadblocks so that you can overcome them one by one. Along the way, you will retrain your brain to catch those nasty repeating thoughts and finally end them!

A *clearer vision*

Creating a life you love is within your power. Visioning can be an invaluable tool to jump-start this process. I used to think that to vision, I needed a big idea. Since then, I have learned that visioning even small goals or habit changes, such as sticking with a daily exercise routine, keeps me on track.

To begin envisioning a life you love, you start with basic questions:

- What is working well in your life?

- What is your biggest challenge?

- What are you learning from seeing that challenge from a new perspective?

- What are some of the small successes you are experiencing? Be sure to record them!

- What can you let go?

Clarity on these questions will jump-start you on your vision path.

What is your overarching theme?

A life theme is an overarching idea that drives your vision. For instance, do you want more personal peace or downtime? Do you want to develop more determination and drive? Would you like more adventure? With your theme in mind, consider the following questions:

- What personal qualities do you already possess that will help you?

- What is your top personal goal?

- What is your top professional goal?

- How do the two fit together?

- What skills will you need to develop to accomplish what you desire?

What is your why?

The question "why" is invaluable. It is essential that your goal be for you and not prompted by what another person wants from or for you. Get clear on this point.

_____

_____

_____

_____

_____

Imagine time has passed, and you have achieved what you set out to do.

- What does your life look like?

- What will you see?

- How will you feel?

- Where will you live?

- What restaurants will you enjoy?

- Does a life you love include the sound of children or horses?

- Will you be listening to wood frogs singing in the woods at night, or will you be performing on the biggest stages in the world?

- Will you feel the sun beating on your skin? Will you hear the ocean?

- When you awaken in the morning, what scents will surround you?

- Who will be sharing breakfast with you?

Get descriptive. Feel into it. This is your future you are envisioning!

_____

_____

_____

_____

_____

_____

_____

How has reaching your goal enhanced your life or the lives of those around you?

If you are not the creative type, have someone help you with this. You want to get all the details down so that you have a solid idea in your mind—one you can revisit over and over to begin making it real.

_____

_____

_____

_____

_____

_____

Imagine you are in your new life looking back at the person you are now.

- What steps did you need to take to get to this incredible place?

- What skills did you develop?

- Have you completed a degree or a certification?

- Have you developed critical relationships and skills you will continue to hone?

- What would you tell yourself about the process?

Be sure to give this time and consideration. These questions will help you plan the steps you will need to take to turn your vision into reality.

_____

_____

_____

_____

_____

_____

How do you overcome roadblocks?
As a human being, there will always be events or the words of others that cause you to become distracted. Using the tools you learned here, such as understanding the negativity bias and how it may affect you, you have the opportunity to analyze your emotions from a more-grounded point of view. Keep in mind that everything is about your perspective—you continue filtering current situations through the emotions you experienced in the past.

Is there a relationship at home or in the office that could use a new perspective?

How might you see the following three examples differently?

- A challenging situation with a family member?

- A demanding boss or frustrating coworker?

- An opportunity that went to a friend when you believed it was meant for you?

Allowing these issues to fester will distract you from your vision!

_____

_____

_____

_____

_____

_____

_____

How might you address this issue?
- Are you comfortable speaking with this person?

- If so, what would you say?

- If not, why not?

- Who might help you work through the issue?

_____
_____
_____
_____
_____
_____
_____

It is critical to your vision to work through your feelings. Feelings are based on emotions that have been fueled by negative thoughts. To bring your vision into being, you will want to keep your mind as clear of negative thinking as possible.

With that thought in mind, consider the following questions.

What repeating thoughts keep you feeling stuck?

_____
_____
_____
_____
_____
_____
_____

How would your life be different if you released this thought?

- What would your relationships look like?

- How would a more-positive thought change your career?

_____

_____

_____

_____

_____

_____

Always continue to bear in mind that taking charge of your thoughts requires time and lots of practice. There will be periods when you find yourself falling back into an old thought pattern or behavior, but don't worry! Falling into old patterns only proves that you are human. Imagine an old thought pattern as a well-worn rut, one that with perseverance you can escape. The graphic below helps me.

During the visioning process, it is essential to measure your wins. Get yourself a journal or a notebook. Commit your wins to paper. They will act as reminders during periods where things are not flowing as easily. Be sure to revisit them frequently!

By following the steps in this guidebook, you can begin building the foundation of a life you love. It takes time and planning, but it's worth the effort.

When you are ready for further help, please visit www.letmylegacybelove.com. Our website offers many tools and courses that will help you along your way, including one-on-one and group sessions. You can also join our mailing list, affording you access to articles, research, and announcements of new programs. If you have found this book to be helpful, I would be incredibly appreciative of an online review. Doing so may offer someone else a chance they didn't even know they needed.

I believe our world needs self-love more than ever. The more you love yourself, the more you light up. As your light gets brighter, your kindness and compassion will act as a beacon to those around you. When your friends and family join in, the light grows brighter and brighter!

Together we can change the world.

You will seek me and find me, when you seek me with all your heart.

—JEREMIAH 29:13 (NIV)

What's Next?

When you first began reading these stories, you may have thought that this book was about me. By now, I hope you understand that it is essentially about my desire to help those who want to live a life they love. I believe that if each one of us makes the time to take a good, hard, and *honest* look at our thoughts and behaviors, together, we can change the world.

As I mentioned earlier, right around the time I finished writing and examining these stories with Carlene, I came across the Adverse Childhood Experience (ACE) Study. This study was initially conducted in the late 1990s by epidemiologists at the Centers for Disease Control using the employees of the Kaiser Permanente Health Plan as subjects.

The researchers were stunned at what they discovered. According to Dr. Robert Anda, one of the primary doctors, the data reveals that those who experienced childhood trauma in its many forms had an increased risk of developing addictions to cigarettes, alcohol, or drugs, and that they often faced ongoing battles with depression, anxiety, and other mental health issues.

In many cases, the stress caused by these issues translated into physical illnesses, such as heart, lung, and autoimmune diseases. What Dr. Anda and the other researchers found even more surprising was that there were just as many professional middle-class Americans affected by adverse childhood experiences as any other group. The good news? Research shows that by identifying sufferers of ACEs earlier in their lifetimes, the adverse effects can be mitigated.

When I took the ACE Test and saw my results, I was excited for two reasons. First, it validated the personal work I had done. Second, since the test is a simple way to pinpoint the origin of childhood experiences that may be at the root of adult issues, I felt it could act as a starting point for others who want to begin their own journey of discovery.

I believe the test may be a helpful tool for others, like me, who don't always find counseling to be helpful. Although I tried counseling several times during my life, in each case, I gave up after five or six visits. Even though the professionals I worked with were terrific people and very skilled, to me it felt like we were examining an *adult* issue, rather than walking me back to the *root cause*. After digging into these stories myself, I now understand that my biggest challenges started in my childhood.

If you are interested in more in-depth information on the ACE Study, you can find links to some sites that I found helpful on www.letmylegacybelove.com.

I believe I have given you a lot to consider. Something may have surfaced that requires closer examination. If that is the case, you have options. As a certified neuro-linguistics programming practitioner, I can get you started. I not only work personally with individuals, I have also developed several courses which are available on www.letmylegacybelove.com. Any of these are a good way to start.

For those who would like to pursue traditional therapy, I found it helpful to ask others for referrals to professionals they appreciated. Since you are a unique soul, it is a good idea to interview a therapist to be sure you are on the same page. About twenty years ago, I made an appointment with a psychologist a friend had suggested. When I arrived for my appointment, he waggled his finger at me to follow him without saying my name, and then not once during our session did he make eye contact. For me, that behavior was a deal-breaker, so I did not continue with him. It is so much nicer to work with someone you feel genuinely cares about your success, and the process is much easier and more fun when you feel a resonance with the person.

I invite you to take the ACE Test which is on the following page. It's only ten questions and takes less than five minutes to complete. It may offer you insight that could start you on a path that will change your life.

I wish you the very best on your 3 Rs path of Revealing, Releasing, and Reclaiming. I invite you to check out my website for programs and events that may be of help to you (www.letmylegacy-belove.com) along the way. I also have two Facebook communities (www.facebook.com/letmylegacybelove and www.facebook.com/ ILoveMyLifeChallenge), as well as a Christina Beauchemin You-Tube Channel and my *Miracles in Everyday Moments* podcast, which is available across all channels.

I am continually developing programs and sharing research that I hope you will find helpful, so when you go to my website, please sign up for my mailing list. We are very respectful of your in-box, so you can be assured we will not be inundating you with messages.

I am excited for you! As you continue your journey to more self-love, please reach out at any time. I love seeing your e-mails each day, and I answer each one personally.

Let My Legacy Be Love!

*Love does no harm to a neighbor. Therefore love
is the fulfillment of the law.*

—ROMANS 13:10 (NIV)

Finding Your ACE Score

While you were growing up, during your first eighteen years of life:

1. Did a parent or adult in the household often or very often swear at you, insult you, put you down or humiliate you, or act in a way that made you afraid that you might be physically hurt?

_____ Yes _____ No   If yes, enter 1 _____

2. Did a parent or other adult in the household often or very often push, grab, slap, or throw something at you or ever hit you so hard that you had marks or were injured?

_____ Yes _____ No   If yes, enter 1 _____

3. Did an adult or person at least five years older than you ever touch or fondle you or have you touch their body in a

sexual way? Or attempt or actually have oral, anal, or vaginal intercourse with you?

_____ Yes _____ No   If yes, enter 1 _____

4. Did you often or very often feel that no one in your family loved you or thought you were important or special? Or that your family didn't look out for each other, feel close to each other, or support each other?

_____ Yes _____ No   If yes, enter 1 _____

5. Did you often or very often feel that you didn't have enough to eat, had to wear dirty clothes, and had no one to protect you? Or that your parents were too drunk or high to take care of you or take you to the doctor if needed?

_____ Yes _____ No   If yes, enter 1 _____

6. Were your parents ever separated or divorced?

_____ Yes _____ No   If yes, enter 1 _____

7. Was your mother or stepmother often or very often pushed, grabbed, slapped, or had something thrown at her? Or sometimes, often, or very often kicked, bitten, hit with a fist, or hit with something hard?

_____ Yes _____ No   If yes, enter 1 _____

8. Did you live with anyone who was a problem drinker or alcoholic or who used street drugs?

_____ Yes   _____ No   If yes, enter 1 _____

9. Was a household member depressed or mentally ill, or did a household member attempt suicide?
_____ Yes   _____ No   If yes, enter 1 _____

10. Did a household member go to prison?
_____ Yes   _____ No   If yes, enter 1 _____

Now add up your "Yes" answers: _____ This is your ACE score.

For additional information on the ACE score, check out our website at _www.letmylegacybelove.com._

ACKNOWLEDGMENTS

What a privilege it is for me to acknowledge the many people who played a role in the completion of this book. I am so grateful to each and every one of you.

First and foremost, I want to thank my friend Carlene Nolan. What an extraordinary gift it was to work with you on this project. When we met in a yoga class in 2006, neither of us could have imagined that nearly ten years later the depth of our friendship would be the foundation of this book. Through the years, we laughed, we cried, we argued, we agreed to disagree all while putting a few thousand miles on our walking shoes. The years spent as each other's support system were some of the best of my life. Carlene, you will forever hold a very special place in my heart.

Margaret Bakowski and Denise Omilian, you have been incredible assets in the process of honing the stories. Your thoughts and feedback made a huge difference. I hope you know how much I appreciate you.

Thank you, Marcia Maxwell-France. Your reminder that patience is the only way to get to the heart of a story was a turning point for me. I am exceedingly grateful to you, my friend.

Juliette Looye, my friend and soul-sister, your editing, thoughtful comments, questions, and reminders are a cause for celebration! What a joy it was working with you.

Amy Moses-Schoenfeld, thank you for reminding me to carve out time for myself to play! Our lighthearted conversations and your gentle reminders saved me from myself on more occasions than I can count.

Mindy Mackenzie, a huge thank-you goes out to you for our weekly mastermind sessions. Our calls helped me to stay on track while I cleared the unnecessary distractions from my life that would allow me to finally write my story. Your wisdom is exceptional. I am honored to call you my friend.

Jennifer Scavina, when you came to me with a proposed book title, "Becoming Christina," neither one of us understood the deeper meaning. Thank you for sage advice, kindness, and prayers.

Thank you, Pascale Daviau, for being my friend, my mentor, and in the worst of times, my rock. I love you.

John Nolan, thank you for your insight and for lending me your wife during your first year of marriage!

Steve Eisner, owner of When Words Count Retreat in Rochester, Vermont, thank you for believing in me.

A huge thank-you to Michelle Vandepas. Your words of encouragement and keen sense of what I was trying to accomplish led me to the title of this book. I will be forever grateful.

To the Enlightened Bestseller team of Marci Shimoff, Janet Bray-Attwood, Chris Attwood, and Geoff Affleck, I offer a million thanks. Your willingness to share your experience and knowledge has been a godsend.

Thank you goes to Joel Roberts, media coach extraordinaire. Encouraging me to write this book from the perspective of the witness was game-changing.

Erin Parker and Jesse Finkelstein of Page Two Strategies, thank you for your comments and thoughtful feedback. Working with you was an amazing experience.

Thank you to Jason McIntosh of 5D Creative for the illustrations. As usual, they were exactly right on the first try. You are truly gifted.

Christofer and Benjamin VanWormer, I can't imagine a greater blessing than to have the two of you as my sons. You've seen me at my worst and loved me anyway. Your encouragement and understanding have made this project so much easier. I am blessed to have you with me on this journey.

I got lucky the day you came into my life, Rick Beauchemin. You are my best friend, and the best husband a woman could ever have. Thank you for your support, encouragement, insight, and, most of all, your patience. I could not have done this without you beside me.

To the many teachers who have passed through my life, I am forever in your debt.

To God, my greatest teacher—I thank you for the many gifts you've bestowed on me and for the people you have brought into my life, just when I needed them most.

About the Author

Christina Beauchemin is an advocate of courage and honesty. She is a motivational speaker and a private mentor who leads programs to assist others in finding peace and forgiveness in their lives. Before leaving the business world to focus on *Let My Legacy Be Love*, Christina was a business professional with a concentration on streamlining processes to promote organizational efficiency.

A classically trained singer/songwriter and a storyteller, Christina performs and teaches voice lessons to young people. She is a contributing author to the #1 Amazon Bestseller *Ready, Set, Live: Empowering Strategies for an Enlightened Life* with #1 *New York Times* best-selling authors Marci Shimoff, Janet Bray-Attwood, and Chris Attwood.

Christina is the mother of two grown sons, Christofer and Benjamin. She is married to her best friend, Rick Beauchemin, and they live in a beautiful rural area in Upstate New York.